CANADIAN
LIVING

D

SELECTED COLUMNS FROM

CANADIAN LIVING

PETER GZOWSKI

WOOD ENGRAVINGS BY G. BRENDER À BRANDIS

In slightly different form, all the columns in this book appeared in *Canadian Living* magazine, 1989-1993.

Canadian Cataloguing in Publication Data

Gzowski, Peter

Canadian Living

ISBN 0-7710-3729-5

I. Title.

PS8563.Z6C3 1993 C814'.54 C93-094329-5

PR9199.3.G96C3 1993

The publishers acknowledge the support of the Canada Council, the Ontario Arts Council, and the Ontario Ministry of Culture, Tourism and Recreation for their publishing program.

Printed and bound in Canada.

McClelland & Stewart Inc.

The Canadian Publishers

481 University Avenue

Toronto, Ontario

M5G 2E9

1 2 3 4 5 97 96 95 94 93

At one of the many parties I didn't attend during the years these columns appeared, someone—a Canadian Living *reader, presumably—approached a colleague of mine from* Morningside.

"Who's the guy Gzowski lives with?" he said.

"The guy?" said my colleague.

"You know—Gill. He writes about him all the time."

"Oh, that's a soft G," my colleague said. "Jill."

Actually, it's Gillian. Gillian Howard. She is not, believe me, a guy. This book, nearly all of which she read in progress—some parts many times—is for her.

TABLE OF CONTENTS

PREFACE

"Other People
Have Experiences . . ."

 ❧

"WHEN I WAS YOUNG, AND MARRIED," I wrote long
ago in *Canadian Living*, "I would no more have thought
of writing for this magazine than I would have thought
of—well, reading it."

But those had been the days (I went on) when I also
thought that salt-shakers filled themselves, that when you
ran out of toilet paper in the bathroom you just yelled,
"Hey, we're out of toilet paper here in the bathroom," and
someone would open the door and throw you a fresh roll,
and that magazines you could buy at the supermarket
were for . . . well, maybe not for "the little woman," of the
sort the telephone company still assumes has nothing better to do than hang around the house in her pretty frock,
waiting for the repairman to find some time in his busy
day, but certainly not for me.

I learned better. My marriage, a good one while it
lasted (notwithstanding my plaintive cries from the loo),
came to an end—my fault, if that matters. I hunkered

down in a furnished flat. Kentucky Fried Chicken and take-out chow mein quickly lost their novelty. The fridge, bare except for half a bottle of flat tonic water, one blue-encrusted lump of orange cheese, two fossilized lemons and something I couldn't identify wrapped in foil, soon depressed me. I bought a frying pan, eggs, green onions, cream, Parmesan cheese and a spatula. One Sunday, before I left to pick up the kids to join the parade at the bowling alley, I essayed a gourmet omelette.

Next chance I had, I bought some salt, and filled the shaker myself. Bought a pepper mill, too, wishing only that the fingers that had held a thousand pool cues were adroit enough to poke the corns through a hole apparently designed by watchmakers. And more cookware and some garbage bags, and laundry soap and olive oil, and all the other things that, as a comfortable young husband, I had thought just came with the house. And then some cookbooks and a spice rack, bay leaves and balsamic vinegar, J-cloths and *sea* salt, and all the other necessities of home, including, somewhere along the way, my first four-pack of toilet paper.

By the time Bonnie Cowan called me, many years later, I had changed my mind about a lot of things, including magazines.

Bonnie had just taken over as editor of *Canadian Living*. Among her first acts had been to run some excerpts from a book I was just bringing out. Now she wondered if I'd like to try my hand at a column. I said I'd be delighted to give it a whirl. I had been, after all, a magazine guy long before I went near a radio studio, and though I'd been earning most of my living at the CBC for nearly twenty years when Bonnie called, I still missed print—still thought of myself, if anyone asked, as a writer who was working in radio for a while.

Besides, the hundreds of thousands of people who took *Canadian Living* home from the supermarket every month now included me.

THIS IS A COLLECTION OF CONTENTMENTS. Except, perhaps, for machines—no, not perhaps; I hate machines as much as they appear to hate me—there are no villains here. There's some nostalgia, I suppose, and maybe, between the lines, a sense of a country that's slipping away. But these are musings on private concerns, not comments on public affairs. On CBC Radio, where I spent my mornings in the years these pieces appeared, I wrestled daily with Meech Lake and Charlottetown, with the GST and the changing of the Ottawa guard. On golf courses around the country, I played games to help raise money for a cause I feel deeply about, teaching people to read and write. Inevitably, those aspects of my life spilled over into the columns I sent in. But in *Canadian Living,* and with Bonnie's blessing, I wrote—write, if I stay lucky— about people I like or admire or, frequently, love; about places I've been and things I've tried; about occasions that lingered in my mind. The column became a kind of haven for me, a respite from the front pages of life. I *enjoyed* writing it, in a way that, in all my years at various keyboards, I've seldom enjoyed writing anything, and, I think, I often tended to look on the world through the lens of my magazine page. As my cousin Jack said once, and I'm sure this is true for nearly everyone who has a regular writing gig, "Other people have experiences; Peter has columns."

SOMETIMES, TO MY SURPRISE, those columns turned out to involve food.

The surprise, of course, came from the fact that someone who had thought Parmesan cheese turned scrambled eggs into *haute cuisine* was daring to publish his culinary adventures in the company of some, if not all, of the best food writers in the country. *Canadian Living,* as its faithful readers know, is many things: fiercely and jauntily proud of its Canadianness (its editors use more exclamation points than anyone outside a comic strip); unafraid, when it wants to be, of such issues as child abuse or date rape; *unbelievably* (!!) helpful on everything from sewing aprons to forecasting the weather. And through the years of Bonnie's editorship, all those qualities, along with its unpretentious common sense, have made it a healthy success story in the midst of a troubled Canadian publishing industry. But first and foremost it is a food magazine. Where its competitors put models or "Women of the Year" on their covers, Bonnie puts melon balls—and outsells the competition by a mile. Furthermore, it is to most other food magazines what the Montreal Canadiens are to most other hockey teams; a person could feed his—oh, what the heck, his or *her*—family for a year from a single issue and never repeat a recipe. Yet once I'd summoned the nerve to offer my own humble thoughts on cooking

—if, that is, someone who is willing to make public his assumption that he is the best barbecue chef who ever lived can be called humble—neither Bonnie nor anyone else at the magazine, not even Elizabeth Baird, their redoubtable food director, was ever anything but supportive.

They may, of course, have been quietly running up batches of my soups and latkes in the privacy of their test kitchen ("tested till PERFECT"), just to make sure no reader would collapse from indigestion or, worse, disdainful laughter. Once, indeed, Elizabeth and I appeared together at a food show in Ottawa, which was for me a little like singing a duet with Maureen Forrester (or dancing with Veronica Tennant, which, as you'll see, I actually did), and Elizabeth showed up with a suspiciously professionalized version of my now-famous beef stew. But if they were checking up on me they never said so, and, over the years, my colleagues and friends at the magazine became my teachers, too. If, indeed, I had a single bit of advice for someone at the same stage of cooking erudition as I am, which is to say closer to egg-boiler than Escoffier and finding satisfaction as much in the experience as the accomplishment, it would be (see my adventures in baking bread) somehow to acquire Elizabeth Baird's telephone number.

BY AND LARGE, everything that appears here is exactly as it ran in the magazine, winnowed from my first five years.

By "by and large" I mean mostly that I've restored some of the cuts that had to be made to squeeze my

monthly ramblings onto a single magazine page—a page,
I am convinced, that grew smaller as the years rolled by.

Oh, I've fiddled a *bit*: reinstated into a line I like about
the North a cuss word I thought at the time (and probably
wrongly) didn't belong in the magazine; tried harder to
call my youngest son Mick, which he prefers, instead of
Mickey; remembered to add cauliflower to my—oops!
guess they didn't test *this* one—cauliflower soup. And
there is, as you'll see, an Envoi, in which I've tried to
bring a few of my stories and heroes up to date. But I've
resisted the temptation to second-guess myself. If Barbara
McDougall, whom I fantasized about inviting to my all-
woman dinner party, is no longer the "person with the
best chance of being our first woman prime minister," too
bad; she was when I wrote it. If, in light of some of the
details of their private lives that have popped into public
since Charles and Diana last came to Toronto (not to
mention one or two of *his* fantasies), I might not be quite
as gaga as I probably appear here, well, too bad again; I'm
sure I'd still say something stupid if I met them.

MAKING THIS BOOK was as happy a task as was hatching
its various components, and if, as I hope, there's a bit
more in the whole than there was in the sum of the parts,
the credit should go to the people who guided me in putting it all together.

One is Edna Barker, who is a—I like to think
my—book editor. As readers of the various *Morningside
Papers* will know—not to mention almost anything else of
mine that's appeared in book form—I have long since

realized that the more Edna pores over my prose the better it gets. And even after Bonnie and her colleagues at
Canadian Living had done their work, I asked Edna to do a
bit of fine tuning, and to help me choose and shape what
might be preserved. I didn't lose every argument I had
with her, though—or, for that matter, with Dinah
Forbes, a treasure of McClelland & Stewart I had not
thitherto been aware of—so any clumsiness or inaccura-
cies that remain are my fault, not theirs.

Another, of course, is the remarkable Canadian artist
Gerard Brender à Brandis, whose wood-block engravings are known and celebrated around the world. I'm
honoured that he has allowed a few of them to adorn
these pages.

Finally—and Edna and Dinah and Gerard Brender à
Brandis will know why I dare to say most important—is
Peter Sibbald Brown. Not unlike Gerard, Peter, a graphic
designer, is one of Canada's best-kept secrets; his work
may well be more appreciated in California than in
Toronto. But his roots and passions are at Lake Simcoe
where he and I are neighbours. We've done a number of
things together since we met, not all of them involving
the consumption of sherry. His taste and craft have
affected everything from the shape of the house I live in
to the look of my golf tournaments. Books, though, are
both his first love and his greatest genius, and I am more
grateful than I can say that my downtown publishers have
allowed him to set my little pieces in the visual context he
thought appropriate—so different, as it is, from the one
in which they originally appeared.

THOUGH WE LIVE just down the road from each other Peter S. B. and I often communicate by fax, an instrument which has, as you'll see, somehow exempted itself from my pattern of frustration with machines. We bounce ideas around, swap gossip or local politics, share things we've clipped from the papers and sometimes just arrange to meet for drinks. Whatever the subject, Peter always signs off, "Cheers."

Let me borrow the sentiment now.

Cheers, dear reader. May the next person to find enjoyment here be . . . you.

ONE

The Hedges and the Cedars and the Peace

My MAILING ADDRESS and, I guess, legal residence, is in Toronto. I live there because I have to. From the over-priced apartment Gill and I rent downtown, which I leave in the mornings when it's still dark, before the paralysis of the first rush hour, I can get to where I work in nine minutes.

But, for several years now, my *home* has been in the country, eighty-eight happy kilometres away, and early every Friday afternoon when my workweek ends, I climb into my car and head, if not for the hills, then for the hedges and the cedars and the peace.

On the way, I shop. In summer and early fall, I stop first at a roadside stand for corn, tomatoes, new potatoes, beets the size of walnuts and, during those all-too-brief weeks in midsummer, fresh peas from the garden. In winter I begin at the florist's, where I pick up a bright bouquet to take the gloom from the dining room table.

After that, my route varies. If I've rushed from the city

too fast for lunch, I stop at Mike's restaurant on the highway—the Highland, according to the sign out front, but
everyone knows it by the name of its Palestinian owner—
for a homemade hamburger in a pita (easy on the hot
sauce) and a cup of aromatic coffee. Some days, I hit the
butcher's next and try to talk Alex, the owner, into selling me some lamb, in spite of his conviction that it's too
high-priced for my budget. Others, I drop in at the booze
emporium, where the manager, who knows my tastes,
will direct me proudly to his newest Australian wine, or at
the bakery (though it's smarter to wait till Saturday morning, when the carrot muffins are still hot from the oven)
for a strawberry-rhubarb pie. Every Friday, I visit the IGA
on the Dalton Road for staples and salad greens (the cash-
iers are no longer puzzled by my proclivity for watercress), and every second week or so I hit the bulk food
store for spices, vinegars, powdered chicken stock and
chocolate-covered almonds.

By the time I've picked up a movie, some ice and
copies of the two local weeklies (the mayor, a former
newspaperman, writes the same column for each of
them, which ensures against scoops but means we get a
fairly narrow, and noncontroversial, range of municipal
coverage), peeked in at Susan Taylor's new craft store to
see if she has sold one of my neighbour's tapestries yet,
and checked the library for new arrivals, I've extended
my travelling time from Toronto by at least an hour. But
my car bulges with goods and goodies, and I'm ready for
the weekend.

The real satisfaction of my shopping trips, though, comes not from what I've bought but from what I've learned. At the florist's, for example (I wish I'd figured out what a great source florists could be when I was a young newspaperman), Connie, while she mixed some Alstroemeria in with the yellow lilies, has caught me up on who's had a baby this week, who's celebrated an anniversary, who's in the hospital. At the liquor store, I've peeked in the collection jar (and added a two-dollar bill of my own) to check on the campaign to build a new dam where the river crosses High Street. Mr. Eustace, the pharmacist, has told me his son Lee can't play golf with me this weekend (too busy with the new girlfriend)—I'd better call Jim, the United Church minister, though not for a Sunday morning round. Mary, the librarian, has told me that she's found someone to do the typing I was asking about last week. Mike, at the Highland, has some ideas about throwing a dinner to raise money for literacy—he saw in the paper last week that the Rev. Jim and I had done a reading for the cause—and Ann, Alex the butcher's wife, whom I've asked for advice on where to buy firewood, has said for the time being just help myself from their pile around the corner.

And so on and so on. The people I deal with in the small-town part of my life are more than just business acquaintances; they're neighbours—friends. Doing my Friday rounds, I visit. By the time I pull into my own driveway, I'm home the way I never am in Toronto, where, after seven years in the same apartment, I still don't know the names of the people on either side of my walls. In the country, I'm a member of the community; I belong.

I don't know how long all this can last. As Toronto's scorching real estate prices have driven more and more people into the exurbs, our corner of the world has boomed. Housing starts double every year, and the portable classrooms can hardly hold the new kids in the schools. Every week there seems to be a new subdivision. In the past two years alone, we've acquired a new children's clothing store, a unisex barber, a Molly Maid, two new traffic lights, four new video outlets (two of them featuring automatic dispensers that take your credit card), a Pet Villa, a bank machine, a fax link to the rest of the world, fifty cents a message—and a place where you can get your computer fixed. Late last summer, the telephone company announced that we'd no longer be able to call each other with only the last four digits of our numbers. From now on, we'll have to dial all seven. But we still have to dial one to call the city. It's still long distance, in more ways than one.

WHEN THE GROOM WORE
PATENT LEATHER SHOES

Two-forty. A Saturday afternoon in June. I am on the main floor of the fashionable Queen's Quay Terminal on Toronto's waterfront, growing more frantic by the second. In spite of the air conditioning, I can feel sweat in the torn T-shirt I threw on so hastily up at the cottage. I am sockless and, as my kids would say, having a bad hair day. Clutching my credit card, I dash from emporium to boutique, and at each counter, cool young sales clerks are giving me the same scary message.

"Sorry, sir, we don't carry them."

"But you don't understand," I say. "My son is getting married at four o'clock."

"Congratulations," the more polite of them offer. "But we still don't have any studs for a formal shirt."

I wasn't enthusiastic about this wedding in the first place, if you want to know the truth.

I was, to make this clear, enthusiastic about the *marriage*. I liked Julia from the day Mick, who is my youngest, brought her around, and in the time that followed, as they became an inseparable couple, I learned, if this is all right to say, to love her. I thought—and think—Mick is very lucky to have found her.

But a big wedding? With flowers and limos and dancing and catering—and formal clothes? Come *on,* you guys, I'd thought. It's a tough world, tough times. You're at the beginnings of your careers. Nobody's hiring. Mick, in fact, picked up an impressive newspaper award for an article he wrote in the Vancouver *Sun* last spring, and in his acceptance speech could say only—and with typical élan—"Gee, thanks. Anybody got a job?"

Whatever the wedding would cost, in other words, they could surely use it on setting up their apartment more than they could on, say, champagne.

Besides, I couldn't help thinking, isn't this all a little . . . er, old-fashioned?

They'd won, though. Kids always win. Their day, after all. I hid my grumpiness, or tried to. And now, a year after they announced their engagement, here I am—what? oh, my Lord—an hour and ten minutes away, and I won't be able to do up my shirt front.

"We do have some diamond earrings," says yet another cool young clerk. "They're $800 each."

It's been like this all week. One party—or rehearsal for a party—after another. I know I'm not losing a son, I'm gaining . . . et cetera. But gee, couldn't we just *do* it? When Mick's mother and I were married, her father gave us $500 on the condition that he didn't have to go to anything.

"You might try the men's clothing store in the Royal York," says the first clerk I meet who looks old enough to have been through this herself.

"No time," I say, "no time."

I hardly slept last night. Started thinking about what I'd say in my toast to the bride and groom. Kept redrafting it in my mind. I, who give a hundred speeches a year. Still don't feel ready. Do you think they'd like to hear about literacy? Do you think they'll mind if my chest shows?

Only on the way down from the lake this afternoon— the day, of course, they've chosen to close the parkway —do I remember that the last time I saw the little box in which I keep my cuff links and studs it was empty. Must have left them in . . . where the heck was I the last time I wore my monkey suit, anyway?

"Do you have a formal shirt with *buttons*?" I ask desperately at the last-chance men's store.

"Sorry, sir, we . . ."

But I am headed for the parking lot. Forty-five minutes till Stephanie the flower girl, my oldest perfect grand-daughter, leads the procession down the aisle.

TEN-THIRTY P.M., same day—though it feels as if a week has passed. The disc jockey has cued up "The Blue Danube." The guests have formed a circle around the dance floor. We have feasted on fresh pasta and rich beef Wellington, strawberry flan and home-made crêpes. Wine has flowed. Toasts have been toasted; laughs have been laughed. At the church, Julia broke into a fit of mixed giggles and tears at the end of her vow, but, when the minister, smiling, seemed about to carry on, insisted on finishing, speaking boldly and with joy. When Mick turned to walk his bride down the aisle, I had to avert my gaze as I flashed him a thumbs-up. Didn't want him to see the tears glistening in my eyes.

I am as mellow as I was frenzied. The wine? Perhaps, though as MC I've saved most of that pleasure for later. Instead, I think it's been the day, the occasion, the gathering of friends and family—and the old-fashioned way it was done.

Now, Mick escorts Julia to the centre of the circle. She is lovely in her mother's gown. Mick is in tails—Mick, who, as his response to my loving toast has reminded us, used to be the teenager in the blue hair, with pieces of foreign metals stuck through his nose.

His shoes are patent leather. On their own in Vancouver, Julia and he have been studying ballroom dancing, and this is the moment they have chosen to show it off.

It is, I realize, exactly the way it should be. An evening of dancing and a lifetime of love lie ahead of them; this is the style in which they should be launched. God bless them both, I think, as "The Blue Danube" swells. The devil take the extravagance.

My studs? Oh, no problem. They were in my shirt. The cleaning lady had washed it for me after its last excursion. She put them back where she knew I'd find them, if only I'd taken the trouble to look.

Bulbs Up!

~

I can't remember when I first realized that Gill had become addicted to gardening.

Gill is my—what? I've lived with her for the better part of a decade and still don't know what to call her. In one of the sprightly private-eye novels he writes about Toronto, Jack Batten has his character, Crang, hear me describe Gill on the radio as "the lady in my life." Crang, who is sometimes too trendy for his own good, is offended by this turn of phrase, but offers no alternative. So Gill is my—well, we live together. Happily, too.

Her full name is Gillian Howard. She works in public relations. She wasn't a gardener when we first got together, though she always—maybe I should have seen the signs—had an uncommon touch with house plants. Things *bloomed* for her. Benjaminas that would drop their leaves if I so much as walked into the room would, under her gentle care, sprout new shoots of tender green. A potted orchid I bought her sent tendrils up the handle of its basket and popped radiant new flowers daily in the dark of winter. A yucca that had withered and sulked under my nervous over-attention grew—seemingly just because she was around—healthy enough to hide a patrol of guerrillas. Our apartment began to resemble the Ecuadorian jungle.

Still, her potential for addiction stayed hidden. In the apartment, her gardening was casual: a few cuts here, a repotting there. Move the African violets closer to the morning sun, and on Sunday evenings carry a watering can from the sink to the creeping jungle, with half an eye on *Murder, She Wrote*. A social gardener, I thought; she could quit any time she wanted.

And then, a few years ago, we found our place in the country.

At first, she kept her passions under control. Like new homeowners everywhere, we concentrated on fixing up the house, spending every penny we could scrape together on more glass, a skylight, a cedar deck—at the edge of which (I realize the significance only now) Gill wanted a vertical trellis. But when the workmen pulled away their last dumpster, the monster was unleashed. Honeysuckle at the foot of the trellis. Impatiens—how deceptively easy they can be—in the shaded beds under the oak. A new bed the size of a refectory table beside the hedge. Forsythia along the gravelled drive. And, that autumn, the first of her bulbs.

I look back now at the journal she began to keep. Bluebells, a few hyacinth, scillas, crocuses and—undistinguished by brand name in those carefree early days—

the first of her daffodils. "A dozen bulbs in amongst the ferns," she has written, "plain yellow with single trumpet." By the following spring, a note of triumph: "Bulbs up! Flower heads showing by April 29."

And now look: twenty yellow irises, thirty snowdrops, forty scillas. Daffodils? A catalogue: rosy sunrise, Mary Copeland, Texas (who names these things anyway?), Thalia, white lion, Mount Hood, ice follies (thirty ice follies), orangery, Prof. Einstein, on and on—bulbs by the thousands (or so it seems). And the simple, gloating "bulbs up!" of her first spring has given way to pages of tightly written, exquisitely detailed notes, each variety's strengths and shortcomings reviewed like an opening night on Broadway.

Meantime, the refectory table has been expanded to a banquet hall. Brimming with delphiniums, hostas, day lilies, lavendula, physostegias (obedience plants to the laity), dianthus (Mrs. Sinkins are the best), phlox and a dozen other genera, the hedge-side bed now takes up a third of what was once our modest lawn. When the daffodils fade, they're replaced by annuals—petunias, nicotianas, nigellas, larkspur, candytuft. Foxglove and liatris reseed themselves. Forget-me-nots and bleeding hearts lay claim to their own corners. Sweet peas climb the trellis, winding through the orange trumpets of the mature honeysuckle. Morning glories try to scale the house. The garden is alive, a seething, perfumed explosion of pinks and whites and purples.

And Gill? Her winter evenings are now spent with her nose in her growing library of gardening books. In April, our mailbox fills, first with catalogues—evenings when she's lost to reverie—and then with seeds and bulbs. Seedlings begin their lives in rows of boxes that edge the apartment's jungle. Through spring and early summer, she kneels and weeds, cuts and trims, composts, replants, brings bouquets of delight to the dining table. Travel, hitherto a necessity, is now a chance to bag new species— once a sprig of crane's-bill from her grandmother's garden in Nova Scotia, which she cradled lovingly in its damp earth as our plane winged us home.

Her addiction is full-blown.

This is, I know, a common story. Gardening has replaced curling as Canada's most popular leisure pastime. What's behind it, as Marjorie Harris wrote in *Report on Business* magazine this spring, is the fact that hundreds of thousands of people like Gill and me, having finished renovating our houses, are turning outdoors, where, as Gill says, we can tinker forever. As one result, the businesses that grow around gardening—from seed houses to bookstores that sell only garden books— are booming.

Marjorie Harris would know, too; she's a gardening addict herself.

Marjorie is also, by the way, married to Jack Batten. Which makes at least two of us who know the joys of having an addict in our lives.

"BY THE WAY, PETER, WHAT ARE YOU DOING NOW?"

O NE OF THE NICEST THINGS about the work I've been lucky enough to do for thirty-five years or so, interviewing for radio or television or walking around with a notebook in my hand, is that it's put me in contact with an awful lot of well-known figures. Some of them, inevitably, have become my friends. They're writers, singers, actors or, like me, broadcasters. A few are athletes—or were, since at least two of my favourites, Ken Dryden and Randy Gregg, are retired. And some are even politicians, though with politicians, who have a *stake* in making you like them, you have to be careful. Not all the famous people I meet, to be sure, are among those I'd choose to spend a week on a desert island with, but a surprising number of them—surprising to me, at any rate, since I'm distrustful of public reputations—are at least as pleasant in person as they are well-known.

I think this is a Canadian phenomenon. Fame here, I think, is different than fame in most other countries.

With rare exceptions—Pierre Trudeau would be one; Margaret Atwood may be another—we don't like our heroes to stand above us, to become what my grandmother would have called "too big for their britches." We like people who are like us: unassuming, polite, even deferential. One of the reasons we made so much of Wayne Gretzky when he still lived here, I'd argue, was that as well as being the prettiest hockey player any of us had ever seen, he was obviously such a nice young man.

In Canada, we don't have what Americans call "celebrities"—people who are, as they say, famous for being well known. Every famous Canadian I can think of, from Pierre Berton to Karen Kain (quick, name me an American ballerina who's as popular in her country as Karen is in ours), can actually *do* something—often astonishingly well. The longest ovations ever received on the late-night television program I used to host went to (1) Maurice Richard (in Montreal) and (here she is again) (2) Margaret Atwood; can you imagine an American audience standing for a *novelist*?

Some of the public figures I admire the most are, in private, shy and self-conscious. They have to fight it. It practically *pains* Alice Munro to read in public (though she does it magnificently), yet I've seen her autographing in a bookstore, spending a few minutes with everyone in the line, getting to know them, giving them a part of herself. Murray McLauchlan likes parties about as much as he likes periodontal surgery, yet on the stage he fills a room with his warmth.

A lot of the people I admire give much more than they

can possibly get from their fame. Maureen Forrester does so many things—she worked unbelievably hard at chairing the Canada Council—with so much grace and good humour that you can forget she is probably the greatest living contralto, in demand all over the world. June Callwood, who could be rich if she just stuck to her writing, instead spends most of her life working for everything from freedom of expression to succour for people with AIDS. The folk singer Valdy, who still has to tour the country every year working an endless series of one-night stands to keep body and soul together, nevertheless seems available for every good-cause benefit you ask him for. So does Gordon Pinsent. So does Timothy Findley. So does Don Harron, who took some time from his schedule last summer to write, with Norman Campbell, a delicious spoof of their own wildly popular musical *Anne of Green Gables* to help some friends of theirs raise some money for a cause (Mike Duffy flew from Ottawa to Charlottetown to be in it). And so do Cynthia Dale and Knowlton Nash and R.H. Thompson and Dinah Christie and a whole lot of other people who'd have every excuse, if they chose, to rest on their laurels or to make some money for themselves.

It's characteristic of famous Canadians, I think—at least the ones I'm writing about—that they like to tell stories mocking their own prominence. Peter Mansbridge, whose face appears nightly on the CBC, tells of being stopped by a traffic cop in Ottawa one evening, when he'd been speeding to an appointment. "*Peet*-er *Mans*-bridge!" said the officer, when Peter rolled down

the window, and then proceeded to introduce himself
and to ask if Peter remembered they'd been Boy Scouts
together years ago. After a few minutes of nostalgia, however, the officer pulled out his book of tickets. "By the
way, Peter," he said as he began to write, "what are you
doing now?"

Bob Rae, the premier of Ontario who took so long to
get over his genuine surprise at being elected, tells of
being taken to an exclusive club in Florida and being cut
by a member who told him she spent "thousands of
dollars to get in here just so I wouldn't have to associate
with people"—socialists, presumably—"like you." And I
remember once, after a golf tournament in New Brunswick, being driven to the Fredericton airport in the car
of Premier Frank McKenna, with the premier and me
in the back seat, McKenna's executive assistant, Steve
MacKinnon, at the wheel and, beside him, my own inval-
uable Shelley Ambrose. It was raining, and someone suggested that, although we were a bit behind schedule,
Steve drive carefully. Someone else wondered, if we did
have an accident, whose name would be in the headlines,
the premier's or—yes, yes, I have a modicum of fame,
too—mine. "Both," said McKenna. "It'll be 'McKenna,
Gzowski, Die with Aides.'"

COUNTRY FOOD

THE FEAST WASN'T HELD until our second-last day in Pond. Soon after, we would head south again—though "south," in this case, meant only as far as Iqaluit, five hours in the friendly arms of First Air, stopping to pick up a mother and her *amauti*-borne infant at Broughton Island. Four hours south and we would still be on Baffin Island.

"Pond" is what we had learned to call Pond Inlet, a community—a hamlet, to use the Arctic term—of some nine hundred and fifty souls, four hundred miles inside the Arctic Circle. We had journeyed there in late spring, when the sea ice was still solid. On the ice, the people of the North had built us a golf course, scraping away the snow to make fairways and "greens" (whites, really, with brightly coloured flags planted in the frozen holes). Our clubhouse would be an *igluvigaq* of snow. Dog teams, fanning out behind the *qamutiks,* would drive us to the tees. Pale icebergs the size of triplexes towered in the background, and behind them, across the glistening white of Eclipse Sound, loomed the majestic Bylot mountains. A group of us had come from the south—the real south this time—to play this game for the second year. As we had last year in Yellowknife, a metropolis by Pond's standards, we would golf in the name of literacy, raising funds by our antics to help some northerners learn to read and write—not only English and French, but their own Inuktitut.

But the golf was for the morrow. Tonight, we had been promised, was the feast.

I was looking forward to it. I am, if truth be told, something of a northern chauvinist. I have loved all my visits to the Arctic over the years, and have never really understood Canadians who've neglected this stunning and unique part of their own country to travel to other continents. It still frustrates me, as I've said before, that so many of the tourists at such places as Auyuittuq National Park are from France or Norway, or that there's a flourishing business in Yellowknife showing the aurora borealis to wide-eyed Japanese. But I am nevertheless baffled by the northerners' reluctance to promote what they call "country food," the fish, meats and other delicacies of their own beloved land. In Pangnirtung a couple of years ago, for example, I remember chewing on a corn-flakes-covered (and overdone) veal cutlet, sitting in a hotel with one of the most beautiful prospects in all the world, while just a couple of miles away local entrepreneurs were pulling in whitefish to ship to the gourmet restaurants of Montreal.

Pond had been no different. We had been happily ensconced in the Sauniq Hotel, owned and run by the local co-operative. Except for the extra blinds on the windows, to mitigate the constant brightness—the sun doesn't set in Pond between April and August—and except, perhaps, for the piles of mukluks in the lobby, we might have been in a southern hostelry. "And how would you like your eggs done?" our waitress would ask at breakfast. And for the evening meal, we would choose from a selection of soup, roasts, vegetables and sweet desserts. Only once had we tasted country food—a dinner of pink and delicate char. The feast would be different. At last, I thought, I can show the *real* North to some of my southern friends.

SIX O'CLOCK. We gather in the lobby of the Sauniq. Nine of us: Randy Gregg, the medical doctor who played five Stanley Cup championships with the Edmonton Oilers; the country singer Colleen Peterson; Pat Mastroianni—Joey of *Degrassi High*, as every kid in Pond seems to know; lovely Cynthia Dale of *Street Legal*; the Olympian trapshooter Susan Nattrass—a world champion, the kids have realized, using a skill that is a part of their culture, too; the rising young superstar of the blues Colin James; the poet Sheree Fitch; my assistant and the den mother of the trip, Shelley Ambrose; and me.

We are all both tired and exhilarated. Our time in Pond, with its unrelenting light, has been a constant turmoil of activity. We are more than ready to eat.

Six-fifteen. We walk—except for Colin—to the

Community Hall, a frame building the size of a small hockey arena at the other side of town. Colin has been working on borrowing a guitar so he can join Colleen in a little after-dinner entertainment. He stays at the hotel, teaching the young Inuk whose instrument he will use a few blues licks as part payment.

Six-twenty. The C-Hall, as people call it, is jammed. On a stage at the far end, Mayor Paniloo Sangoya prepares to greet us. The other three walls are lined with people. On the floor, spread out in a giant U, is our feast. It is country food. *Boy,* is it country food. Caribou, raw and frozen raw. Char, raw and frozen, including some disembodied heads and tails. At the open end of the U is the greatest delicacy of all: freshly slaughtered seal, the meat as red as rubies, the organs a purply brown.

Six-twenty-five. After the mayor's welcome and an Inuktitut grace, the people fall to. They carve the rich meats with their *ulus,* traditional "women's knives" used for skinning and other household chores, and eat the servings with their fingers.

Cynthia, Pat, Susan and the others are momentarily taken aback, but one by one they step forward to sample the various treats. To my knowledge, only Randy, the hockey player, and Sheree, the poet, try the seal. Everyone looks, shall we say, nonplussed. It is a long way from fettuccine Alfredo.

Six-thirty-five. Colin arrives. I study his expression as he watches Titus Allooloo, a member of the Territorial legislature, relish a scrumptious piece of raw caribou. Maybe, I think, we should go back to the hotel for a bite—except all the hotel staff, including the waitress who brings us our morning eggs, are now squatting around the U, helping themselves to raw protein.

Six-thirty-seven. Phew. We have found a table in a corner, spread with foods more familiar to our southern palates. The caribou here has been made into a stew; the char is cooked—one boiled, one baked. At one end there is even a casserole of rice. And, best of all, plates and forks. We load up. Pass the Diet Pepsi.

TWO DAYS LATER, the plane to Iqaluit circles over our golf course. Just beyond the largest iceberg, two Inuit walk one of the white fairways, bearing golf clubs we have left behind. There are smiles among my fellow tourists. We have brought, we realize, some hints of the pleasures of our gentle game to this awesome, rugged land.

In June, our course will melt and disappear forever. The memories we take with us, I know, will last much longer.

The Eggs and I

We are discussing, Bonnie Stern and I, whether to put egg whites in the tiramisu.

This is a matter of some seriousness. On the one hand, the recipe we are working with, Bonnie's own, *calls* for egg whites, six of them, to be beaten and folded into our zabaglione. On the other, she is reluctant to use raw eggs in any form. There's just too much salmonella around, a much more serious bacterium than most people realize, as she points out now, and Bonnie, who is as health-conscious as she is skilled, doesn't want to take any risks. In her recipe, in fact, she substituted whipping cream for the whites.

Still, the eggs we're using are from hearty, free-range chickens—*all* Bonnie's ingredients are chosen with exquisite care—and the tiramisu is my special request. I want it to be perfect.

As she almost never does when she is teaching or

demonstrating in her kitchen, Bonnie pauses for a moment of deliberation.

I AM, I SHOULD POINT OUT, having a little treat for myself. As my interest and pleasure in cooking have grown over the years I have wanted more and more to understand what I'm writing about, to get better at it. This session at Bonnie's cooking school in Toronto is part of my plan. It's one-on-one—even one-on-two, since one of Bonnie's assistants hovers in the background, scraping the pots and keeping the knives clean, ready at a moment's notice to run next door for, say, whipping cream, while I am the only student, standing at the chopping-block counter, wrapped in an apron, bumping my noggin on the pots suspended overhead and, from time to time, sitting at one of the desks usually filled during Bonnie's classes, taking notes. The menu, with its Italian accent (I am better at eating Italian food than at cooking it), is my choice, picked from a long list of suggestions I've been sent by Bonnie, who can, I am convinced, cook in all the languages of the world.

I'm having a wonderful time. Bonnie teaches as zestily as she cooks, chattering happily all the while, pausing to admire a texture or soak up an aroma. We are well into our second hour now, the first having been consumed with the preparation of an osso buco, which now browns merrily in the oven, spicing the kitchen with wafts of garlic and onion, carrot and thyme, lemon peel and—a typical Bonnie touch, this—pancetta, a rolled Italian bacon, which we have browned with the stock. Later, while the tiramisu chills, we'll work up an appetizer of crostini rustica, grilled bread spread with a garlicky mixture of beans and greens and topped with pitted black olives, and a risotto—romaine lettuce, green onions, Italian parsley and chicken stock (among other ingredients) stirred into the short-grained rice—to go with our main dish.

I am learning at every stage. We have, as I would not at home, planned our time, deciding, for example, that since there are onions in both the osso buco and the crostini, we'll do all our chopping at once. Even as she chops, Bonnie gives useful advice: *roll* the knife (which she holds more like a pencil than a tennis racquet, by the way), use the *dull* edge to peel the carrots, *cross-hatch* the onions first. She shows me a simple slip knot ("I couldn't do this so quickly if I hadn't learned as a child") as we tie the veal shanks to hold in the marrow, and later, when we need some lemon juice, how to squeeze a lemon over my hand so my fingers catch the pips. My head spins. My notebook, when I have time to scribble, fills.

Along with all the tips, and perhaps more crucially, I am absorbing Bonnie's attitude, her infectious pleasure as she repeats rituals she must have been through a thousand times, her occasional flashes of inspiration—"I think a touch of rosemary would help, don't you?"—and the extra touches that make her dishes come to life. When the veal has browned, for instance, she deglazes the pan with a dry white wine, assiduously spatula-ing every delicious brown speck into the osso buco. Moreover, I note with delight (for I have the same reckless habit myself, with less authority), she almost never measures. Three tablespoons of butter? She whacks off a piece from the pound. A cup of wine? She splashes it straight from the bottle. "Just practice," she says when I query her, "though when I bake, I measure *exactly.*"

IN OUR DISCUSSION of the tiramisu, I have taken up the cause of the egg whites. I feel like living dangerously, I say, and add that I feel a proprietary interest. We have separated the eggs together, but it's I who have been charged with whisking the yolks, some sugar—we use a bit less than the recipe calls for—a splash of cognac and some Marsala into a creamy custard. (Yet another Bonnie tip: since store-bought double boilers have flat bottoms, make your own with a metal bowl on top of a pot—but *never* let the bottom touch the water.) Reluctantly, Bonnie concedes. And now, while I begin beating the creamy mascarpone cheese into my custard—neither of us can resist a quick lick from our fingers—she stands over the egg whites in the still-warm metal bowl.

We have waited too long. The whites have begun to cook.

Bonnie says, "Well, we could make a meringue."

But both of us know the matter has been settled.

"It's a sign," she says.

"A sign," I repeat, knowing a lesson when I hear one.

We send out for whipping cream.

DONNA AND CLARENCE,
CLARENCE AND DONNA

∾

Donna williams was twenty-nine when I met her, and Clarence Asham was forty, but except that they were both young adults who were well into new stages in their remarkable lives, and that they left an indelible impression on me, they had almost nothing in common.

They'd certainly never met. Donna has never been to Manitoba—she's Australian, though she lives in England now—and Clarence has never been out of it. He was raised in an institution in Portage La Prairie. He's blind, and what people who are supposed to know about such things call "severely handicapped." At one point, his IQ was measured at thirty-eight, which is not much higher than a German shepherd's.

Donna is autistic, though it took the people who raised her—her family, mostly, but a lot of experts, too—a long time to figure that out. At various points she was thought to be deaf, or "retarded"—or insane. That's more common than you'd think with autism, which affects about four out of every ten thousand children. Autistic kids turn in on themselves. They don't answer questions and can sit for hours staring at the wall or rocking themselves in monotonous and sometimes self-destructive patterns. They're almost impossible to get through to. In Donna's case, it didn't help that she'd been abused at home.

Clarence was abused, too. Even in the institution he was the butt of jokes. He took to biting, and had to be segregated. He was put in a ward where everyone else was dying. He didn't speak.

I MET THEM BOTH, on the radio, in the same month.

Donna—this is incredible when you think of her background—was on a publicity tour, promoting a book she'd written about her life. Clarence was at a house in Winnipeg, where he'd been living for the past five years. We hooked up a line to the living room, and, before we talked, listened to him playing the piano.

Neither was what you might call a routine interview. Before Donna and I sat down to record anything, she came to the CBC to meet me, to get accustomed to my voice. I had to be careful not to wear bright colours— purple, in particular, is almost physically painful to her— and to speak simply, and take my time. Words, as she explains (her book is called Nobody Nowhere), are a jumble to her. It's as if she can tune in only one sense at a time, and whatever channel she's on—sight, or sound, or even smell—is so powerful it almost overwhelms her. At one point, I told her I thought my work with literacy might be a bridge for us. "But I'm the *opposite* of illiterate," she explained, in her halting spoken prose. For her, speech can be total confusion, but writing was the key to her freedom. She wrote her book in four weeks, just letting her feelings pour out. "I wanted to see what kind of mad I was," she says. But the first psychiatrist who saw it recognized it for what it was: a work of brilliance and importance, the gateway to an unknown world.

Clarence's key was music. He's a "musical savant." In the institution, an attendant taught him some elementary accordion. Soon, Clarence was outplaying his teacher, all by ear. He picked up the piano and began reproducing what he heard on the radio. It's amazing. He can play anything, from Brahms to Bacharach. Some psychologists who've studied him figure he has more than two thousand tunes in his head. On the radio, he played the *Morningside* theme on the accordion (he'd never heard it before), then, when I invited Paddy Maloney, the leader of the Irish musical group the Chieftains, who'd been waiting in the wings to talk with me, to come in to the studio and bring his penny whistle, Clarence joined in on a sprightly mazurka.

If music was the key, the locksmith was Lillian Doig. Lillian is in her fifties, a widow who raised her five children in Edmonton, moved to Winnipeg to be near the eldest and found herself in an empty house. When a friend—her minister, as it happened—asked her if she might think of taking Clarence in for company, she said, "Sure, why not?"

In the house, Clarence has blossomed. Once, early in his time with her, Lillian found him whimpering in his room. She couldn't figure out what was wrong. Stomach pains? Headache? Finally, she discovered the batteries in his Walkman were dead. "Don't cry," she told him gently. "Just say, 'Lillian, fix it please.'" Two days later, his closet door was jammed. He called to her. It was the breakthrough. When I asked him if he knew he was on the radio, he told me "CBC," and laughed, then added, "nine-thirty in Newfoundland" for good measure. He told me the score of the previous night's hockey game, too, and imitated the organ with his accordion.

An IQ of thirty-eight? I don't think so.

MY INTERVIEW WITH DONNA was just as moving. We talked for nearly an hour—at first with me asking questions I'd written out for her in advance, but then, for a long time, just out on a limb, with Donna sitting quietly on a piano stool, away from the light, concentrating on every word. She talked—I can still remember the words—about "buzzing under a pink street light" or being able to see the different greens of every blade of grass. Throughout, I couldn't help thinking, she saw things I didn't see, understood things incomprehensible to me.

DONNA AND CLARENCE. Clarence and Donna. I wondered, after I met them, how many others like them there are, people in prisons not of their own making who, if only someone could find the key, might also break out on their own.

My Daughter the Author

The children of my now long-dissolved marriage —that's funny, isn't it? children, when their ages total 148 years—*look* quite a lot alike.

Both the girls have the same gorgeous red hair, which they got from their mother's side, though one, Maria, has almost always worn it long and the other, Alison, shorter. The boys are all within a quarter inch of the same height, and I would guess, weigh within a few pounds of each other. Alison and John have the same high foreheads and—I think, anyway—aristocratic noses, and Peter and Mick are almost indistinguishable from each other on the phone, except Mick, the youngest, may be even cheekier than his older brother.

They all have similar outlooks on life, too. They're bright (if I may say so), irreverent and funny, though they're all—except, perhaps, for Mick, who has a touch of the class clown in him—also rather shy.

Looking at them, in other words, or talking to them

for a while, you can easily figure them as siblings.

In other ways, they could scarcely be more dissimilar. One, Peter, the eldest, studied engineering chemistry at university, and now works at the keyboard of a computer, figuring mathematical formulae that are beyond normal comprehension. Another, John, is a jazz guitarist and composer, who skips around the country playing festivals and after-hours clubs, while a third, Maria, is the stay-at-home mother of my two perfect granddaughters. Only the other two have chosen careers that have in any way followed mine. Mick, after dropping out of high school—that wasn't far from following in my footsteps, either, come to think of it—and spending a few years working as a roadie for rock groups, among other jobs, bit the bullet a few years ago and signed up as a mature student at journalism school. This summer, a few years older than I was when I started at the Timmins *Daily Press* nearly four decades ago, he begins his first job as a newspaperman. And Alison, who is the second oldest even though I've left her here for last, this season published her first book.

Are all families like this? My guess is they are—or were, before having more than 1.2 children became something that made people whisper about you. (What's going to happen to all those big houses we lived in, anyway?) Some kids take after their mothers, some after their fathers, and some—where John got the genes to be a *jazz musician* (he's good, too), no one can figure out—just take off on their own.

God bless 'em, I say. One of the rewards of parenthood

is its sheer unpredictability. Kids go their own ways, surprising you at every turn, and the harder we push them in directions we'd like them to take, the harder they resist. I remember when Peter, still in short pants, was a promising chess player. I took him downtown, to show him off for some experts. He did well, too. But he had a miserable time. It was my idea, you see, and not his. (Not long after, he gave up competitive chess altogether.)

Whatever successes our children achieve, in other words, are *their* successes, not ours. They are no more reflections of what they've inherited from us than their shortcomings—should they have any—are our fault.

ALL OF WHICH, of course, explains why I was so cool this spring when Alison's book hit the stands.

Or would explain it if I'd been cool.

Instead, I was more excited than I can remember being about anything since I held my own first book. On publication day, I held Alison's work in my hands, turning it over and over in wonder and admiration. I rubbed its dust jacket, sniffed its pages, pored over its cover design, teared up over its dedication—"For my parents"—and checked its pagination. I marvelled at the way its designer had put her full name on the spine: Alison Gzowski, as opposed to just the surname, which appears on my works, and which will differentiate it in the bookstores. I thought of the author's tour, the glamorous cocktail parties, the fawning reviewers, the adoring fans, and someday—why not? —the Governor General's Award. Still daydreaming, I tucked the book (it's called *Facing Freedom: The Children of Eastern Europe*) under my arm, and took a leisurely stroll around the office, hoping someone—anyone—would stop me to ask what I was carrying.

"Why, it's a book by my daughter," I would say. "My daughter, the author."

FACING FREEDOM tells the stories, largely in their own words, of adolescents who spent their childhoods behind what we used to call the Iron Curtain and who are now, well, facing freedom, with fascinating results. Alison worked on it for a year and a half, which started when she went to Czechoslovakia to teach English, and then carried on as she travelled through Germany, Poland, Russia and Latvia. In the process, she did all kinds of things I'd never do: rolled up to high schools and simply asked to meet kids; rode subways through cities racked by street gangs; braved the gunfire of Riga under siege. Then she transcribed all her interviews, and worked them up into book form. When she had a draft finished, I looked it over, and made a suggestion or two—there has to be some point in having a father with eleven books of his own under his belt—and she did a bit of repair work. Then, *voilà*—my daughter, the author.

Even though, for a first book, *Facing Freedom* has done remarkably well, Alison may have to wait a *bit* until she gets her first best-seller, and none of my fantasies for her future have come true yet, either.

She has had one cocktail party, though. I threw it. All

her brothers showed up, too. Her sister? Maria was busy that evening. Stephanie—*her* oldest daughter—was in a school concert.

And wherever Stephanie's musical talent came from, Maria must have been very, very proud.

THE BELLTONE AMP

❧

I AM SITTING at a crowded table in, of all places, a
nightclub. Like the middle-aged couple next to our party,
he in a ponytail, or the people of various ages draped over
the bar, their costumes ranging from grunge to business
suits, I am intent on the music.

The sound from the stage is low-key and intricate. It's
jazz, to be sure—the club we are in, the Top of the Senator, is a showplace of Toronto jazz—but there are overtones of non-American cultures in it, strange (to my ear,
anyway) blends of India and the Orient. Guitar, cello,
saxophone. Two sets of percussion. The players are serious, and the crowd, except for bursts of enthusiastic
applause after each long number, is serious, too.

I have come here reluctantly. Neither jazz nor night-
clubs are particular passions of mine, and the hour is long
past my bedtime. But the music is getting to me. I find
myself tapping my toes to the prancing rhythms of the

bongos and following the flights of invention and dexterity on guitar and cello and sax.

I am also swelling with pride. The handsome young man on guitar, who is also the composer of the piece we are listening to now and—though the musicians seem to play collectively, more like a string quartet than a band— the leader of the group, is my second son (and fourth child), John, a rising figure on the Canadian music horizon. Tonight marks both the launch of the first recording of his group, Mecca, and the opening of their four-night engagement at an important jazz venue. I am very glad to be here.

I'VE WRITTEN BEFORE about how unresponsible I feel for my children's various accomplishments. I'm proud of all my kids, and lucky to have them. But their successes are theirs, not mine, just as their shortcomings (in the unlikely event they have any) are not my fault.

John, obviously, proves the rule—a jazz musician for heaven's sake, the son of a man so musically inept he has it written into his radio contract that no visiting performers will get him to hum the bass parts.

And yet and yet, I muse as Mecca's music washes over me. There is, after all, the Belltone amp.

IT STARTED WITH a ukulele and, I think, "If I Had a Hammer." The uke came from a music store. "If I Had a Hammer" was in the Pete Seeger songbook that came with it. Somehow—"My Dog Has Fleas"—I learned to tune the plastic strings, and on Friday nights, with the

book open in front of me, Harry and Penny Bruce and John's mother and I would sit around and belt out, "If I had a (change) hammer, I'd (change) hammer in the morning," and, "If I had (change) wings, like (oops, change again) Noah's dove," and, "How many (change) miles must a (change) man walk down," and a whole hootenanny of other songs that were in the air then.

Then, of course, was the sixties. *Everyone*—even young married couples with growing families—played guitar. I bought mine for about sixty dollars and, slowly and laboriously, following, this time, Pete Seeger's instructional record, learned to finger enough chords to fake it through our Friday singsongs. G, D^7, C, A^m, E^m, B. I'd sit by the record player for hours on end, slowing Pete down while I tried to follow him through the melody of "Little Boxes" or the chord patterns of "House of the Rising Sun."

Neither lack of talent nor an ear of tin discouraged me. I bought *more* instruments. Banjo (Pete taught me—or tried to—to "hammer on"). Twelve-string guitar (as hard to tune as to play). And, when Bob Dylan went electric, so did I, with a black and silver guitar, complete with whammy bar and, to the despair of everyone else in the house, a tangerine-coloured Belltone amplifier, the size of a small suitcase.

And that was that. As suddenly and as inexplicably as I'd started, I stopped. The instruments, the instructional records, the books—even the piles of old *Folkways* magazines—went into the basement, along with the shell of my tropical fish tank, my unthumbed chess books, my squash racquet and other souvenirs of vagrant passions. When, a decade or so later, our marriage ended, I left them all behind me.

THE WEEK BEFORE his gig at the Senator, John and I were talking about something else.

I don't think, in fairness, I've ever realized how good he is, though an awful lot of the young musicians who troop through *Morningside* are more impressed by the fact that I am John Gzowski's father than that I have a regular job of my own. Oh, I've seen him do the music for a souped-up *Rigoletto* and attended a recital of dances for which he was a composer. But his world is so remote from mine that he's beyond my ability to judge. He's *stratospheres* above my musical knowledge. He builds his own instruments, among other mind-boggling accomplishments, including a guitar for which he's split the octave into nineteen equal tones. He may well be, as a grizzled old jazz guy I know once told me matter-of-factly, a genius. But to me, I blush to say, he's just quiet, gentlemanly John, as nice a young man as I know—with a single-minded dedication to his art.

But then, when we were talking, he happened to mention another job that was coming up. He'd be playing with Meryn Cadell, he said, the brilliant and original young singer who's well on her own way to stardom. They'd be on *Friday Night! with Ralph Benmergui*. I might want to watch with special care, John said. The amp he'd be using might look familiar. It was the Belltone, in all its tangerine glory.

THE AGING VOLUPTUARY
COOKS ALONE

❧

Friday evening. The Aging Voluptuary's lady is working late. His children, adults all, are busy doing what he used to do himself on Friday nights. The Aging Voluptuary has had a hard week, and now, alone in the house, he is feeling sorry for himself.

Ah, well, he thinks. At least he will be in undisputed control of the television, and he can zap from channel to channel without causing what the police he covered as a young reporter used to call "a domestic."

Now, what to eat? The layout of the Voluptuary's kitchen provides a clear view of the television. Usually on Fridays, after the AV has done the shopping, he and Gill cook and watch television together, the Voluptuary working on the main dish while Gill tosses a salad. As they work, they comment on the day's events. It makes for a pleasant way to begin the weekend, culminating when the AV brings his latest masterpiece to the table.

Tonight the ritual seems empty. The Aging Voluptuary, who has come to cooking late in life, delights in its pleasures. But, he realizes, as he stares forlornly at the refrigerator door, much of the satisfaction comes from the shared results. On his own, he is inclined only to barbecue a pork chop and microwave a vegetable or two in chicken stock. Cooking for himself, he still believes, is cooking for sustenance only. This afternoon, with the prospect of a solitary evening, he has not even bothered to shop.

Gloomily, he checks the contents of the freezer.

Hmm. The remains of a box of outrageously expensive shrimp he bought in the summer from a man who comes door to door (anything to make him go away). Half a package of scallops, all, significantly, slightly different in size; a Maritimer once told the AV that if frozen scallops were all exactly the same they were likely to be not scallops at all but pieces of skate, punched out with a cookie cutter. Whether this is true—or ever was—the AV still believes it, the way he still believes you shouldn't refreeze ice cream.

Shrimp and scallops, eh? Maybe he can work something up. A stir-fry? No, he has it—a pasta sauce. There's always extra pasta in the Aging Voluptuary's house, since supermarkets sell it in packages too big for one dinner, too small for a banquet. It's like the hot-dog buns, which are never in sync with the number of wieners. Sure enough, in a cupboard above the stove, just behind the peanut butter, is half a package of linguine.

The AV turns on the television. The news has almost

finished while he sulked, but he realizes he'll be able to watch the game shows that follow without having to brave Gill's disparaging remarks. His spirits are picking up.

He pokes around for more ingredients. Good, a red pepper in the crisper, a bit wrinkled, but what the heck. On another shelf, a package of snow peas. And, best of all, in the drawer where the AV keeps his bulb vegetables are, along with a healthy cluster of garlic, five firm shallots. Shallots, sweet and gentle little sisters to the onion, last only a week or two in their lonely darkness—better care-takers than the AV wrap them in paper towels in the fridge—and that they're still fresh this evening confirms his decision about what to cook.

Also in the refrigerator—aha!—half a bottle of Hille-brand Chablis, light and airy on the palate, $5.65 at the liquor store. The Aging Voluptuary has long since con-quered his prejudice against Canadian wine—especially at $5.65 a bottle. As the theme from *Jeopardy!* trills from the television, he pours himself fifty cents worth and leaves the bottle on the counter. A splash, and maybe a gurgle or two of cream, will add the finishing touches to his seafood sauce.

He puts a pot of water on to boil for his pasta. Later, since he's alone, he may fling some strands of cooked linguine at the refrigerator door to see if, as he has read, they stick when they're *al dente*; in company he would never dare.

Maybe cooking for one is not so terrible after all.

He puts the shrimp and scallops in the microwave and

sets the dial at thaw, slices the wrinkled pepper into man-
ageable chunks, nips the ends off the snow peas and peels
and dissects the shallots. With the garlic, he takes a whirl
at being Graham Kerr, the Galloping Gourmet, who used
to chop garlic on television with the speed of a wood-
pecker. Where Kerr chatted at the camera while he
worked, the AV watches a round of *Jeopardy!*

Oops. Forget Graham Kerr. The Voluptuary needs his
fingers for typing.

Another sip of the Hillebrand. The ding of the
microwave signals the seafood's readiness.

Into his favourite heavy-bottomed pan, with the heat
on medium high, the Voluptuary pours a generous glug
of extra-virgin olive oil and adds a solid chunk of butter.
While the butter melts, making swirls of abstract beauty
in the burnished gold of the oil, he contemplates spices.
Ginger? Dill? A touch of cayenne? He savours the
essences in his mind.

Working swiftly now, he sautés the shallots and garlic to
aromatic softness, scrapes in the peppers and snow peas
from the chopping board, slips the stiff linguine into the
boiling water and finds a wooden spoon to blend the flavours of his ad-libbed sauce. He slides the thawed shrimp
and scallops onto the colourful bed of sizzling vegetables,
and, just before splashing in the wine, raises his glass in a
silent toast to the television.

HOMEMADE THEATRE

THE FIRST (and so far only) time I heard a *Canadian Living* joke in the theatre was early this summer in Blyth, Ontario. The play was a piece called *Local Talent* by the Montreal playwright Colleen Curran, and it was having its world première at the opening night of the sixteenth annual Blyth Summer Festival—a gala event that had every one of the five hundred seats in the old Blyth Memorial Hall jammed with people in summer dresses, jackets and ties, and here and there, shorts and brightly coloured shirts.

The *Canadian Living* joke wasn't all that great, to tell you the truth. Just something about one of the characters, an entrant in the baking contest in the Mrs. Canada Pageant that was the centre of the play, having won Best Chicken Recipe of 1988 in the magazine's pages. But the people in their summer dresses and bright shirts laughed anyway, just as they laughed at other jokes, about the CBC, about the Musical Ride, about one of the characters—another Mrs. Canada contestant—appearing in a dress made out of a Canadian flag, and most of all about yet another woman in the play saying, with lung-bursting pride, that wherever everyone else came from she came from "Brussels, Ontar-i-ar-i-o," which is, of course, just down the road from Blyth.

They were all—we, actually, for I was one of the people in jacket and tie—having a very good time.

MY OWN MEMORIES of summer theatre go back nearly half a century to a storied night at Lake Simcoe, when a touring production of Shakespeare got caught in a power failure. Unabashed, the audience moved outside, brought their cars into a semicircle, turned on the headlights and, mosquitoes and all, the company finished the last couple of acts.

In the years that followed, I witnessed the rise and—far too often—fall of myriad companies of summer stock. I had many happy evenings. But, by and large, I came to think of the old hey-kids-we-could-put-the-show-on-here kind of theatre as irrelevant—a pleasant piece of nostalgia. As more and more cottages plugged into cable television or installed VCRs, the standard recipe of British suspense and recycled Broadway comedy just couldn't compete. There were some exceptions, of course, but the only sure successes, or so it seemed, were lavish productions of imported classics at such festivals as Stratford or Niagara-on-the-Lake.

I reckoned without Blyth, where, to a degree unimagined even by the people who founded it, an extraordinary lesson in what Canadians will watch if you serve it up to them has unfolded.

BLYTH IS A TINY FARMING community in rich and gently pretty Huron County, a few miles inland from the shore of Lake Huron. Its most imposing architectural feature is its Memorial Hall, built seventy years ago—the opening was marked by what the local paper called "a calithumpian parade"—to honour the veterans of World War One. Although it had a long history of housing everything from minstrel shows to Scottish concerts in its auditorium, by the spring of 1975, its roof was in disrepair and there were some feelings the hall had had its day. That's when a freshly graduated theatre director named James Roy began talking with Paul Thompson, the founder of Theatre Passe Muraille. Roy had spent part of his childhood in Blyth, and Thompson had staged a Passe Muraille play in the hall. With the support of Keith Roulston, editor of the Blyth paper, they decided to make a tentative try at reviving the old auditorium.

For safety's sake, they put on yet another production of Agatha Christie's *The Mousetrap*, a hoary thriller that still holds records for longevity in most of the world's theatre cities. But for their own satisfaction, they also commissioned a dramatization of *Mostly in Clover*, a memoir by Harry J. Boyle, who had grown up in St. Augustine, an even smaller Huron County farming community down the line.

Mostly in Clover outdrew *The Mousetrap* nearly three to one.

Blyth, a festival of *Canadian* plays, has never looked back. There were sixteen performances that first season. This year, before the festival closes in mid-September, there'll have been more than a hundred. Five different plays—three of them premières, all of them Canadian—will be seen by nearly fifty thousand people, and after that the Blyth company will take to the road. In town, some eighty people—nearly a tenth of the population—now work for the theatre, and sixteen hundred from the county are signed up as patrons, subscribers or proud members of the board.

At first, the great hits were about the life of the Blyth region: a dramatized Alice Munro work (Ms Munro lives in Clinton, also in Huron County), Passe Muraille's *Farm Show* (also set in Clinton), the brilliant series by Dan Needles about life on Wingfield Farm, even a play about the nuclear installations in neighbouring Bruce County. But the more the festival's founders stretched their audience—there was a breakthrough when local farmers responded enthusiastically to a poetic work from Alberta—the more the audience was willing to stretch its horizons. Now, Blyth does plays from and about virtually all parts of Canada—including, in these troubled times, translated works from Quebec.

What has happened, of course, is that the people of Huron County—and more than seventy per cent of the audience comes from within a hundred miles—see themselves on the stage. When they do that, they laugh and applaud and sometimes cry and nearly always come back for more.

I'll be doing that myself, I know, even if the *Canadian Living* jokes aren't very good.

Imagining Dinner

W HEN THE WOMAN who was my boss turned fifty a couple of years ago, a friend of hers wanted to throw a dinner party for her. "Fine," said my boss, "you can come since you're organizing it. But no other women. I want all my guests to be men—and men of my choosing."

Nice idea, eh?

Nice party, too—I know from having been one of the guests. Ever since, I've been looking for an excuse to hold a similar affair myself—with, of course, the ratio of the sexes reversed—and I've spent hours making lists of possible invitees. Herewith, my fantasy dinner party guests, ten Canadian women (I couldn't stop at six and am too superstitious to go to twelve) I'd like to spend an evening with. I submit it, you'll note, in alphabetical order. Even I don't have the nerve to choose who sits next to whom.

1. Mary-Wynne Ashford, a doctor in Victoria. In an earlier incarnation, Mary-Wynne, who's also an accomplished writer and actor, was a doctor's wife (she has three

children), but when she was thirty-eight she decided she'd had enough of that and went to medical school herself. Now, in another relationship, she both practises medicine and heads up the Canadian division of Physicians for the Prevention of Nuclear War.

2. Maude Barlow, political consultant and feminist (Trudeau had her join his office to deal with women's issues), who lives in Ottawa, where she ran unsuccessfully for Parliament and now chairs the fiercely nationalistic Council of Canadians and fires off lively bulletins on everything from defence policy to free trade.

3. Debbie Brill, the high jumper (and author) from British Columbia. Once, on the radio during the Ben Johnson scandal, I asked Debbie, who has represented us with grace and skill around the world for nearly two decades, if she'd ever taken or been tempted to take, steroids. "Are you kidding?" she laughed, and all of a sudden, during the darkest of those days, I felt better.

4. Dinah Christie, the singer and comedienne. In a country that knew better how to treat its stars, Dinah would be up somewhere around Carole Channing. In Canada, she lives on a farm in southern Ontario, does a little Noel Coward here, a little cabaret there and is always available to help good causes.

5. Nellie Cournoyea, minister of resources in the Northwest Territories. I first knew Nellie when she was a CBC station manager in the Mackenzie Delta, where she was born and grew up, and though she's since become a key figure in the slow but important devolution of political power from Ottawa to the people of the North,

I still know how human she is under the exterior of a driven politician and how quickly, in her deadpan, *sotto voce* way, she can cut through the doublespeak of the world she lives in now.

6. Evelyn Hart, a principal dancer with the Royal Winnipeg Ballet. This has been a year of sorrow for Evelyn, with the sudden and tragic deaths (in unrelated accidents) of Henny Jurriens, the RWB's artistic director, and David Peregrine, her long-time dancing partner. But she is a woman of unquenchable spirit (as well as matchless beauty in her art) and she will, somehow, overcome.

7. Dulcie McCallum, a "mature Anne of Green Gables," as she's been described, who was working as a public health nurse on the Queen Charlotte Islands when she decided she could achieve more by becoming a lawyer, and now she practises law, mostly in the service of people with mental handicaps, in Victoria, where, for all I know, she swaps yarns with Mary-Wynne Ashford.

8. Barbara McDougall, the federal minister of employment and immigration, the minister responsible for the status of women and, right now, the person with the best chance of being our first woman prime minister. Barbara (I knew her years ago, when she was selling stocks and bonds on Bay Street in Toronto) smokes cheroots; what else need I say?

9. Alice Munro, the author. I know, I know, it's Margaret Atwood who's supposed to be the queen of CanLit these days, and whose reputation glitters around the literary world. But I like Alice: shy and hesitant in

conversation, but also saucy, flirtatious—and, at auto-graphings (which she loathes), generous and attentive to her fans. She can also write like an angel.

10. Margaret Somerville, director of the McGill Centre for Medicine, Ethics and Law in Montreal and a member of the National Advisory Committee on AIDS. Dr. Somerville—she has a post-graduate degree in pharmacology as well as being a lawyer—may well be the smartest woman in Canada. In the work she does at McGill, sorting through the thorny questions raised by the leaps of science, she may have to be. She's also among the cheekiest and most outspoken.

Cheek, irreverence and the courage of their various convictions are, in fact, characteristics all my guests share. All are accomplished, bright, and, as I happen to know from having interviewed them on the radio, capable of making me laugh even as they make me think. In this age of women's achievements, indeed, the only person who might be out of place at my party is the host. But, what the heck, it's my idea, isn't it?

Excuse me for a moment, while I open the wine.

CONFESSIONS OF
A TREE-KILLER

❧

No ONE KNOWS FOR SURE how old The Tree is. Our best guess, my neighbours' and mine, is that it was planted sometime in the 1870s by Frank Sibbald, a scion of the family that used to own much of the land around our place. Still does, as a matter of fact. One of the first people to show concern when The Tree got sick was my friend John Sibbald, the Squire as we all call him, Frank's (I think) great-nephew, whose own holdings stretch for hundreds of acres.

Whatever its precise age, The Tree has stood for more than a century, a white pine that marks the meeting of our driveway and the road. It cools the house in summer and, in winter, shields it from the howling winds.

I don't know how tall it is, either. I tried to triangulate its height one day this spring, when we were out seeing how many bulbs the squirrels had eaten and marvelling once again at the rebirth of the garden. But when I stood on the road, holding a ruler at arm's length and squinting at The Tree, all my understanding of high-school trigonometry disappeared in a swirl of cosines and hypotenuses. I gave up. Let's say eighty feet, anyway. Maybe more. It's tall as a castle. Majestic. It would have been nearly as tall, I sometimes think, when my grandfather walked past it on his way to get the mail.

Now, I know, it won't outlive me—even if I don't quit smoking. This saddens me. If I pass this small corner of the countryside on to my granddaughters, the corner of the driveway will be marked by only a sprouting birch, or roses that climb The Tree's gnarled stump. The sun will glare unbroken on the roof; ice storms will blast the walls. What's worse is that The Tree's early death will have been, if not my fault, then a result of my misguided priorities.

IT'S SIX YEARS NOW since we bought the place that has become our retreat. It was a bargain then, a small blue cottage on half a lot on the Hedge Road in the cottage country of southern Lake Simcoe. Even when I was a boy, summering at my grandparents' place nearby, the Hedge Road was the area's best address, a quiet, cedared enclave between the lake and the golf course. Stephen Leacock and Mazo de la Roche are buried in the churchyard at one end of the road; at the other, just before you hit the commercial bustle of Jackson's Point, is the Briars, the Squire's place, one of Ontario's most elegant resorts, its main building an expansion of the old Sibbald mansion. By the mid-1980s, the Hedge Road had been discovered by escape-bound and prosperous Toronto. Prices shot up. Nearly all the airy, white clapboard bunga- lows I remembered from my boyhood were winterized, refurbished as—or sometimes replaced by—more sturdy board-and-batten, and many of the old families who had taken the train from the city for weekends, or whose wives and children spent their summers at the lake while the husbands sweltered in the city, had given way to com- muters or the retired.

We, as I say, were lucky. The blue cottage had some- how escaped the suburbanization of the Hedge Road. We bought, as they say you should, the least prepossessing place on the best street.

We, too, decided to renovate. With a designer friend and my cousin Jack, we made our plans. Jack hired three Finnish craftsmen and set to work. Down came the old blue walls, and up went a glassed-in clerestory. We closed in the back with golf-ball-proof windows, and sur- rounded them with cedar decking. Gill, the chatelaine, began to plan her garden.

And I insisted we bury the wires.

For decades, the hydro and the telephone had come into the blue cottage overhead, strung from a pole on the road. I wanted them underground, to fit the style of our renovated house. Jack called the hydro. On a day the Finns weren't working, subcontractors gouged out a ditch deep enough and wide enough to have formed part of the Maginot Line. At the base of the tree, they chain- sawed through roots as thick as pythons, leaving scarred and naked stumps to gasp for nourishment in the cold spring air. Nearly half the root system was pulverized. The Squire took sad photographs of the deserted battlefield.

WE HAVE TRIED, over the years, to nurse The Tree back to health. Arborists who have served the Sibbalds since John's father's day came running after the wire-buriers had wreaked their havoc. They pumped the wounded root system full of fertilizer and ran steel cables from its branches into anchors in my understanding neighbour's lawn—a far uglier imposition than the wires we had sought to hide. One summer, a specialist from far-off Oakville clucked sympathetically, talked of the old pine in human terms—"one trauma like that makes it susceptible to other shocks"—and dotted its lower half with taps of mysterious chemicals; for weeks, the lower part of The Tree looked like a woman with curlers in her hair.

But every year it grows more desperate. The branch that reaches highest is now almost devoid of green. Branches of branches are grey with death; the twigs are black. In fall, the driveway fills with brown needles. The cars that whiz along the Hedge Road may soon be in danger from falling limbs. From the golf course, where I interrupt my play to cast guilty glances upward, The Tree looks pale and sickly against the sky. It is doomed.

THIS SUMMER, I know, we'll have to cut it back. But The Tree rises with its own lovely architecture, and the

removal of any of its major branches—there are seven—
threatens its symmetry and balance. Sooner or later we
will have to take it down.

We do this all the time. We run to the countryside to
find surcease from the cities, and then impose our city
values on the land. Some day, if we don't change, we'll
run out of nature to ruin.

The Tree is just an example. I wish there were someone
else to blame.

GARBAGE

THE FIRST SIGN I SAW that there might be a garbage dump in the part of the country where I have spent my happiest times was, literally, a sign.

I'd been away. I couldn't wait to get back to the lake. Drove up the bustling freeway that seems to creep a little farther north each year, bringing the city ever closer. Turned onto the narrower highway. More farmland now, and, since the recession, the pace of construction has slowed. Still, this stretch has changed immeasurably since my grandfather used to chug up for weekends in his old Morris Minor. Traffic lights. Restaurants. Great rectangles of development, rows and rows of identical houses reaching over the horizon. Shopping malls.

Our community—I was approaching it now—is called, officially, Georgina. Our local weekly is the *Georgina Advocate,* and our mayor—a former editor, who still writes a column—is the mayor of Georgina. But no one I know *lives* in Georgina. We live in Sutton and Jackson's

Point, Keswick and Pefferlaw, Roches Point and Willow Beach and (yes) Egypt, and on the highways and concession roads that link them.

Much of it, in my day, has become commuter country. On Monday mornings, if I dare to sleep over, I pull out into a steady stream of headlights pointed south. The Mac's on the Dalton Road stays open twenty-four hours, and the busiest counter is where they keep the coffee machine, with three sizes of cardboard cups and lids, plastic thimbles of cream, paper packets of sugar, cellophane clumps of doughnuts. John, one of the butchers in the shop next door, remembers when my grandmother, on weekdays when the Morris Minor was in the city, used to make her shopping trips into Sutton by canoe.

The sign that tipped me off was right at the corner where I turned for home. "NO DUMP," it said, in hand-lettering. In my ignorance, I thought at first it was just a warning to people not to deposit their refuse in that particular farmer's field. But there was a sign on the next property, too, and the one after that, and on and on, on virtually every laneway and gatepost. "STOP THE DUMP," "FIGHT THE DUMP," "WE DON'T WANT TORONTO'S GARBAGE." They'd sprung up like asparagus.

What had happened, I soon learned, was that the province had just published its report on possible sites to store Toronto's overflowing garbage. For years, everyone had known that, sooner or later, the provincial metropolis would just run out of room, and this was it. Sooner or later was now. A committee of experts had looked around and said, okay, what about here, or here—nineteen possible locations, and two of them were in Georgina.

Not all the signs were hand-lettered. Even in the earliest days of the campaign, people were forming organizations, the most notable of which, whose distinctive black-and-yellow signs were to become as familiar as lupines in the Maritimes, was GAG, Georgina (the different towns and villages were coming together now) Against Garbage.

OVER THE SUMMER the campaign grew steadily more furious. Front-page editorials in the *Advocate,* steaming letters to the editor, more citizens' groups, rallies. The dump was practically all people talked about at Foodland or the IGA ("If I see those inspectors coming up the road, I'll shoot out their tires," said one dairy farmer I know), and people called each other all the time with the latest developments. The local cable TV channel, ordinarily restricted to white-on-blue listings of AA sessions and flower shows, came to resemble one continuous town meeting. Nearly every lapel in town sported a button in GAG's black and yellow, telling Ontario's minister of the environment, whose department was behind the scheme, to "Dump it in your ear, Ruth Grier."

The anger wasn't confined to our neighbourhood. Every other community on the list (the long list would be boiled down to three, then one) was upset. If Ruth Grier, who had gone into politics in the first place to fight an incinerator in her own back yard, was not the least popular politician in Ontario, I don't know who was.

THROUGH IT ALL, I was troubled.

Garbage dumps—landfill sites, to give them the name that doesn't quite make you hold your nose—*are* a nuisance. The technology that surrounds them is probably better than we think, but they *do* attract sea gulls and other unwanted visitors; they *can't* be good for the water supply. And even if they are at the cutting edge of scientific knowledge (can you think of *anything* that's turned out to have *less* harmful consequences than the technocrats have predicted?) the mere act of filling them involves thousands of trucks roaring up and down the roads at all hours of the day and night. And, like everyone else, I sure as heck don't want one near me. Dump it in—well, someone else's ear.

But the garbage has to go somewhere, doesn't it? We may call it Toronto's—and if you think this situation is unique to southern Ontario take a look at what's piling up near you—but it's hard to imagine all those commuters who head south every morning, their cardboard coffee cups perched on their dashboards, coming back in the evening with all the messes they've created during the day neatly wrapped in their trunks.

No, it's *our* garbage, really—all of ours. It's all those cardboard cups and plastic creamers, all that cellophane and extra wrapping, all that—*stuff*.

It's not the politicians we should be mad at, you know. It's us.

THE JOYS OF
SISSY SCRABBLE

ல

Iт'ѕ FAIRLY TYPICAL of the way Gill and I play Scrabble together that at a crucial point in one of the hundreds of games with which we've whiled away so many rainy days over the years, I was staring in frustration at the letters in my hand: C, O, blank, B, I, E, S.

"COOBIES?" I mused aloud.

"I don't think so," Gill said.

"Maybe COLBIES," I said. "Or COSBIES—they're some kind of television award."

"Those are Casbys," Gill said. "And that would be a proper name."

"Nuts," I quipped.

Gill paused for a moment. By now, of course, the letters I was poring over were clear to her.

"CORBIES," she said.

"Isn't that a whiskey?"

"They're ravens," she said.

"Ah," I said, turning to the *Scrabble Dictionary*. "There

it is: 'CORBIE, *n* pl -s a raven or crow,' right between 'CORBEL, *v* to provide a wall with a bracket,' and 'COR-BINA *n* a food and game fish.'"

The blank went on top of Gill's AVE (*n* pl -s an expression of greeting or farewell) to make RAVE, and CORBIES, reaching a double-word space, scored me a cool eighty points, including, of course, fifty for using all seven of my letters.

"Remember that," Gill said.

"That corbies are ravens?"

"No," she said. "That I gave it to you."

AT SCRABBLE, Gill is a formidable opponent. She's an amateur naturalist, with an apparent knowledge of every faun that ever gambolled and every flor that ever bloomed. She's also a former English teacher *and* a crossword puzzle aficionado, which means that along with her abundant vocabulary of real words she knows about COSes and TORs, OBIs and OBEs, and EFTs and ERNEs and ERSes. (An ERS, in case you were wondering, is an ERVIL, and an ERVIL is a VETCH.)

Fortunately for the evenness of our long-running Scrabble series, she is not quite as strategically minded as I am—not, dare I say it, quite so cunning. As she does in all games, she plays more for the joy of the moment than the thrill of the chase. She plunks down a selection from her mental thesaurus, and chuckles with pleasure as she racks up her score. I, on the other hand, hoard and scheme, saving my Ss as if they were diamonds, building a store of

INGs and REs and IONs, keeping my Qs and Xs until they can bring me a multiple score.

Occasionally, as a result, I can beat her.

AS YOU'LL HAVE FIGURED OUT by now, Gill and I play sissy Scrabble. In our games, there are no challenges, and you can look up your word before you actually play it, although you are not supposed to go what we call "shopping"—to look for words that begin with, say, KAR (KARN, KAROO, KAROSS, KARROO).

This appalls Scrabble purists, who think (and they have an argument) that half the fun lies in taking chances, either in playing a word you *think* exists—and risking losing your turn if you're wrong—or gambling that your opponent is bluffing.

But it suits us. We bought our first *Official Scrabble Players Dictionary* some years ago, a paperback, which we thumbed till the Zs turned to tissue. Then, last Christmas (I can't remember who gave it to whom), we invested in a newer, hard-cover edition, which, as the earlier work did not, recognizes ZIT (*n* pl -S, a pimple) if not ZEN (ZITI, by the way, is a tubular pasta), and QAT as the name of a shrub.

Even for those of us who abide by it, the dictionary can be annoying. It recognizes UNIQUER, for example, though as anyone who's ever worked on a newspaper knows there are no degrees of uniqueness. It takes QUA but not QUO, EF (the letter) but not EE, and it's full of idiosyncracies. But (1) it's the world's greatest single repository of two-letter words—AA, OE, AG, UT and OD (a hypothetical force of natural power) among them— and of Q words that don't need US (QAID, QANAT, QIN-TAR and QOPH, along with QAT), both of which add immeasurably to Scrabble's pleasure and your scores— and (2) it settles *all* arguments; a word is either in there or it isn't.

Our game suits our friends, too. Scrabble was invented in the 1930s, but it didn't catch on until the '50s, when someone put it into Macy's. Since then, in my family's houses at least, it's withstood the onslaught of everything from Canasta to Trivial Pursuit, and since Gill and I resurrected our board a few years ago, we've been amazed at the variety of people we know who enjoy it—though occasionally, as in the case of Gill's mother, we've had to force them to play by our sissified rules. Murray McLauchlan plays Scrabble, and so does his wife, Denise Donlon, the head of MuchMusic. So do Diane Francis, editor of the *Financial Post,* and my CBC boss, Patsy Pehleman, and David Staines, editor in chief of the New Canadian Library (though Gill, to his chagrin, took him to task at our rules), and, it sometimes seems, half the other people I know.

The best player I've ever met—better even than Gill, she cheerfully admits—is Kevin Peterson, publisher of the *Calgary Herald.* Kevin has an intense running Scrabble match with Catherine Ford, the *Herald'*s associate editor, and an even more intense one with a little portable set he has nicknamed Monty. Except by Monty's computer (and occasionally by Catherine) he's unbeatable. But on at least one rainy day this summer, I've vowed, I'll tackle him again.

Will I quit if he beats me? As the corbie quothed, "Nevermore."

THE CENTRE OF THE UNIVERSE

H<small>E IS AN OLD MAN NOW</small>—eighty-three, I am to learn later—and he leans on a cane as he stands before me.

His eyes are smiling, waiting to see if I remember who he is. Before the name comes to me—wait, wait, it's at the tip of my mind—I see the athlete's grace in his bearing, and remember the smoothness of his swing.

Summer. It was in the summer. I was twelve, maybe thirteen. I had my first full-time job. The man who ran the canteen at the golf club had signed me on as a dogsbody: for two dollars a day, seven days a week, I would ride my bike down the Park Avenue hill, under the spreading shade trees across from Dickson Park, with its empty barns awaiting the candy-flossed glamour of the fall fair, across the old stone Queen Street bridge, pedal up Water Street, between the red brick CPR station and the towering granite of the GCI—the Galt Collegiate, where I would go next autumn—and out the Preston highway to the golf course.

I would begin the day by mopping the shower-room tiles, stuffing the soggy towels into hampers, then I'd sweep the locker room, rinse out the tin ashtrays and pack the green beer bottles into cases. When the canteen opened, my boss, a fat man with a constant cigarette drooping from his lips, would leave the serving of coffee and chocolate bars to me and go to check my work. On Wednesday afternoons and weekends, when the doctors and the businessmen made up their foursomes, we would stock the pop cooler with Black Horse and O'Keefe's, and sell it illegally—thirty-five cents a bottle, I think—to the thirsty golfers, my stepfather among them, a bit embarrassed by his prepubescent bootlegger at the till. When I rode home through the summer dusk, my hands would smell of hops and barley, where beer had sprayed from the bottle opener on the cooler's side.

I hated it, as only a kid can hate his first job.

But sometimes in the morning lulls or when the threat of rain kept the course empty, I would wander from my basement lair and up to the pro shop by the first tee. There, the man who stands before me now would smile his gentle smile and let me take one of the clubs down from his display and go outside and swing it.

"Want to hit some?"

He had an English accent.

"Well, sure, but I . . ."

"Go ahead," he would say. "There's nobody coming for a while."

His name—I have it now—is Art Hunt. He liked kids, and gave a lot of us his game. Some of his pupils went on to become champions, for he could teach as well as he could smile. I didn't, as it happens—even if I'd had the necessary gifts, he wouldn't have had time to polish them; I left both the town and junior golf not long after that summer. But now, as he stands before me, leaning on his cane, the memory of his kindness rushes back.

I AM, THIS WINTER AFTERNOON, in a bookstore, flogging a book, a collection of letters to the CBC radio program I host, and the line-up that passes by the table as I sign seems to be stepping right out of my childhood.

This is Galt. The sign at the city limits says Cambridge, for long ago the government of Ontario consolidated it with nearby Preston and Hespeler under a neutral name. But it's Galt to me. I lived here from the time I was five, when my divorced mother married Reg Brown of the Narrow Fabrics Weaving and Dyeing Company Ltd. on Spruce Street, until I was fourteen, when she died.

And now, like the words in my old school scribblers, the past comes tumbling back. Two places behind Art Hunt in the line-up is Jim Chaplin, bearded now (as, after all, am I), but when he throws back his head and laughs I remember the time our junior basketball team beat Kitchener, and wild nights at the drive-in, where we went in the car his father, the Tory MP, would let him drive. Jim is president of the family firm now; I wonder if the kids still make the same jokes about its condoms as we did about its, uh, French safes. Then Tom Brown, who lived two doors down from us on Park Avenue, now head of the jewellery store run by *his* father, in whose dusty

back room I folded boxes all one Christmas holiday, earning pocket money to buy my mother a present. And
Jeanette Chippindale—Jenny Grieves, as she was in grade
three—with whom I spend a few moments of nostalgic
delight, rhyming off the staff of Dickson school: Miss
Zavitz, Miss Hewlitt, who, with her sister, lived on the
first floor of our Park Avenue duplex, Miss Durward—
still alive, Jenny says—Mr. MacInnis, the famous Pop
Collins. Charlie Wilson, next in line, is now principal of
the GCI—"running the asylum," as he says. Tom Wright,
who makes me try to guess his name (I can't), is in real
estate. And here's David Graham's wife (David lived next
door) bearing a picture of a couple of dozen of us in full,
childhood-fantasy football garb (mostly breeks and
hockey sweaters) posed by the Galt *Reporter*—"the rag,"
as it was to us—by a concrete wall in Dickson Park; there
are two Band-Aids on my face in the picture, my fantasies
of play having involved being tough enough to be
injured. And a man who lives in the old Keachie house,
and someone who practises chiropractic in the building
that once was the Carnegie library where my mother,
the children's librarian, read Kipling to some of the kids
in the football picture, and Shirley Brown, Reg's niece,
on whom I had a cousinly crush, and someone else with
a commemorative pin in Dickson's school colours (we
were blue and gold, Central was red and gold, St.
Andrew's white and gold and Manchester, on the tough
side of the tracks, was black and gold—St. Patrick's,
where the Catholics went, was green and *white*) and, best
of all, Mr. Ferguson—Frank Ferguson as the world calls

him now, but Mr. Ferguson always to me—a Mr. Chips among English teachers (best in Ontario, the province said when he retired in 1964), who was allowed to teach at the GCI in spite of having been a candidate for the CCF and whose crowded bookshelves hold the published works of several former students, among them me. Mr. Ferguson bends closer to hear my reminiscence of the time he turned his class into a debate on . . .

The memories won't stop.

THE BOOK I AM FLOGGING is *The Latest Morningside Papers.* Among its twenty-eight chapters are two on the subject of going home—going back, with fresh eyes, to places the authors of the letters once knew well. The letters in those chapters were written, as many of the letters to *Morningside* are, in response to some ruminations of my own. But the subject of *those* ruminations, I cannot help thinking as I sit here now, signing the title page, was a visit to Moose Jaw, Saskatchewan, a city where, though it affected me profoundly, I worked for less than a year.

And this place, unmentioned in the *Papers,* is my real home town.

I wasn't always happy here. My mother's second marriage was rocky; the stress affected my youth. I have seldom been back since I left and, as the chapter in the *Latest Papers* illustrates, I have written much more about less consequential parts of my life than the years I spent here.

But the time I have spent in the bookstore has opened floodgates to streams of childhood memories I cannot now shut out.

It's time to leave; the next stop on my book tour beckons. I pack my souvenirs.

But I'll come back for a proper visit someday soon. These are good people. Under the scar tissue of the memories I've tried to shut out are happy times.

Everybody comes from somewhere. Me, I come from Galt.

CONCENTRIC CIRCLES

Because my mother remarried after her divorce, I had, when I was a kid, more names than most of my friends. Other than that, I think the lists I used to write on the flyleaf of all my scribblers were just my version of what every kid wrote, and which, unless the world has changed, they still do.

My lists went: Peter John Gzowski (and for my stepfather) Brown, Upper Duplex, 24 Park Avenue, Galt, County of Waterloo, Province of Ontario, Dominion of Canada, Continent of North America, Western Hemisphere, The World, The Universe.

Remember? My guess is that you did it, too. We wrote our lists as if all creation stretched out in concentric circles from where we huddled. They put a claim on our own corners. *There,* they said for each of us, *among all the variety of existence, this is me; this is my space.*

I've been thinking about those lists in the weeks and months that have led up to the hundred and twenty-fifth summer that Canada has begun, at least, as a nation. Two thoughts stand out for me.

One is how much many of the items on my list have changed. The house at 24 Park Avenue, for instance, has become a single-family dwelling; there is no "upper duplex" any more. There's no Galt, either, except in the hearts and minds of those of us who grew up there. It's now part of something called Cambridge. There is an Ontario, though my stepfather, who insisted that CCF stood for "Cancel Canada's Future," would be astonished to see who's running it. But who would say "Dominion" of Canada these days, and who thinks of living in the Western Hemisphere? As for the Universe or, as we sometimes wrote, the Galaxy, our ideas about what's out there have been altered immeasurably.

My other thought is subtler, though it, too, is about change. In the days when I wrote in scribblers, if you'd asked me which of the entities on my list *defined* me—which of all those concentric circles was the *important* one—I'm quite certain I'd have said Galt, one of the places that has disappeared. Oh, I knew I was a Canadian. My father, after all, was overseas, fighting for Canada. But if you'd asked me where I *came from,* I'd have said Galt. North America? I hardly ever thought about it. If I felt a part of any international configuration, it was the British Empire, splotches of distinctive pink, in those days, on the maps on our classroom wall. And citizenship in the hemisphere, much less the world, was an idea whose time had not yet come.

That's changed. In 1991, half a century later, if you

asked me the same question, I'd reply, without hesitation, the circle around Canada. I live in Toronto, province of Ontario, and so on (it used to be in the county of York but isn't anymore) to the edge of known space. But it's as a *Canadian* that I think of myself.

What I wonder, as this troubled and troubling summer begins, is to what degree I am an exception. I have been, after all, extraordinarily lucky. The years after Galt have taken me all over this country. After university (as I've said before), when all my friends were going to Paris and London and Zagreb, I went to Moose Jaw, Saskatchewan. I still pound the same beat. Nearly all the work I do has a *Canadian* constituency as opposed to a local or a regional one. (I still haven't been to Paris, either, except the one on the Nith River in Ontario.)

Other people, I'm sure, have other priorities. If you asked *them* to pick the defining circle from those that emanate from *their* lives, you might get a lot of different responses. In Quebec, for example, the answer is clear—at least among francophones. Without using my circular figure of speech, some pollsters asked them this very question a while ago. An astonishing majority said they thought of themselves as Québécois first and as Canadians hardly at all. I don't know of similar polls in other parts of the country (though it might make an interesting study). But my guess would be (and you might want to try this on yourself before reading my assumptions), that in Newfoundland (which joined us politically, don't forget, only in 1949, and then by the barest of margins) more people would define themselves by their island than their

country; that in Nova Scotia, New Brunswick and Prince
Edward Island it would be a toss-up between the individual provinces and "the Maritimes"; that in Ontario—at
least southern Ontario—Canada might win (Ontario still
has the unfortunate habit of thinking of itself *as* Canada),
but that in Manitoba and Saskatchewan it would be, at
best, *western* Canadians; that in Alberta it would be either
the same or as Albertans, and that in British Columbia it
would be—well, I remember Jack Webster, the mighty
broadcaster, once wondering whether I could succeed
him as a talk show host in British Columbia and saying,
"Nah, you think there's life on the other side of the
mountains." Canada would be on the lists, in other words,
but most people—or certainly a heck of a lot of them—
would choose a smaller circle as being more important.

And this leaves out the people—environmental
activists, for example—who now *would* call themselves
citizens of the world, or the free-traders who are simply
North Americans, or, for that matter, those who through
sexual orientation ("I'm gay") or physical difference or
racial origin (not many aboriginals now call themselves
Canadians) would pick their defining characteristics from
a very different list.

Am I wrong? Maybe. It's guesswork, as I say. But as I
look out from the centre of my circles I see example after
example in the rest of the world of what we used to call
nations drawing larger and larger *economic* boundaries
around themselves (the European Market, to choose only
the easiest example) and at the same time, smaller and
smaller *cultural* ones (the Baltic republics of the former

Soviet Union). What's been happening in Canada is not really so out of sync with the rest of the world as some people have suggested.

And if I'm right? Well, maybe it isn't so awful, after all. We've been going through the most dramatic soul-searching in our history these past few months. It *has* been a troubling time, and some of it has hurt. But it's also been exhilarating. We've at least been looking at ourselves; we've reconsidered our concentric circles. My suspicion is that, as we've done that, we've begun to realize how important the Canadian circle is. As the wise old journalist and author Bruce Hutchison told me, "We're coming to our senses." We may not all want to put Canada at the top of our lists, but we don't want to take it off, either. The circles are, after all, concentric, and our understanding of them does change.

Happy Canada Day, 1991.

TWO

THE HOUR OF
THE LARK

It's five o'clock. The birds, having sung the night into submission, are quiet now. The sun won't rise—officially—for another forty minutes, but I can already make out the silhouettes of cedars on the golf course. A soft breeze sways the browning branches of a spruce. It's still grey out, but clearer every time I look. Now an oak limb becomes a crow, preening himself for the day's first engagement. The railing on the deck is coming into focus. The orange pink of honeysuckles adds a splash of colour to the screen. Across the way, the white of birches stands out along the woods. The horizon lightens. Black cedars turn to forest green. A warbler flutters. Two squirrels hop across the lawn. It's lighter still. Slowly, at God's own pace, the morning is taking shape.

I've been up for some time, working at my puttering. For nine months of the year, these early wakenings are my duty. Now, in summer, they're my pleasure. To the astonishment of almost all my friends, who figure that any

rational person who gets a chance to sleep in will, I rise
early by choice. More often than not, I open my eyes
before the sound of the alarm, which in my working life is
set to ring at 4:14 A.M. (I like a little symmetry in my life),
but for these summer days is half an hour later, like Newfoundland. I pull on the handiest old clothes—shorts, if
it's warm enough—brush my teeth, grind some coffee
beans and, while the coffee perks, head out by car for the
morning paper. (It still bemuses me that country folk, of
which I'm one in summertime, will drive to do errands
city dwellers walk for.)

Circadian rhythms? Maybe. There *are* such things, I
know. Gill, for example, could sleep in the mornings
through a dress rehearsal of the Musical Ride, and the
coffee grinder whirs with impunity. But whatever the
physiological evidence, I am convinced we set our own
internal clocks; we *choose* to become either larks or owls.
As a teenager, I snoozed away with the best of them. But
one year at university I worked on a newspaper shift that
began at one in the morning and ended at nine, just in
time for lectures. With no alternative, I learned to hit the
sack in the early evenings and rise at midnight. Ever since,
I've been able to adjust my sleeping pattern to any setting
I want, and this one, rising before dawn, is my ideal.

Am I nuts? Again, maybe. Even if I nap in the afternoon—I'm grumpy as a Kodiak when I clamber out of
those interludes—I'm not the best of company after, say,
nine-thirty in the evening. I leave other people's dinner
parties right after the zabaglione, and when we have
people in (which is my idea of the best way to spend a

social evening anyway), I've been known to disappear even earlier—"Don't let me keep you up," I say as I climb the stairs.

Culturally, I'm a bit impoverished. Johnny Carson could have retired in 1978, for all I know, and until the CBC considerably moved its evening newscast to nine o'clock, about the only time I ever got to see it—not to mention the late innings of baseball games whose beginnings I'd watched the night before—was when it was replayed in the early mornings, between the advertorials for car wax and the black-and-white Vincent Price movies. Other than matinées, I haven't been to the theatre or the ballet since Jan Rubes was a soprano.

But look around me now. The last of the mist has lifted from the golf course. A solitary player, my morning acquaintance for years—we've never met, but share the brotherhood of early mornings—pushes his cart through the dew. A hummingbird hovers at the honeysuckle, while the neighbour's cat stares in frustration from the grass. Sunlight chases the shadows from the deck. If I touched the railing now, I could feel the first comforting warmth. The roses on the trellis are sweet with scent. In the garden, Gill's lilies turn their faces to the climbing sun.

Indoors—it is close to seven now—I have finished the paper, concentrating more on the cryptic crossword than the politics, and checked the television for the baseball scores, the weather and, as always, the possibility of *real* news among the litany of pestilence and disaster. "Other than the weather," asks Neil Postman, in his incisive *Amusing Ourselves to Death,* "when was the last time you heard anything on the radio that affected the way you spent your day?"

Bill McKibben, in *The Age of Missing Information*—by far the best book on television I've read this year—goes even further than Postman. McKibben, whose last book was called *The End of Nature,* lives in upstate New York, but to write about what television has done to our lives he taped every minute of every program for twenty-four hours on one of the most crowded cable systems in North America, the embodiment of the Bruce Springsteen song "57 Channels (and Nothin' On)." Then, after studying his findings—it took him almost six months of full-time watching—he went alone to a mountain top. In his book, he contrasts the two experiences, and argues (I'm simplifying) that by thinking we absorb everything from the tube—Americans now watch seven hours of television a day, and Canadians aren't far behind them—we in fact absorb very little. There's just too much of it: too much trivia, too little context. On the mountain top, he sensed the real world again: the changing seasons, the feel of rain.

Here, on a summer morning, I know what he means. The big stories are all around me. The shrinking rain forests? I *know* there are fewer songbirds than even five years ago. The hole in the ozone? Watch the grass on the golf course turn brown again this year. The population explosion? Here, where I sit, used to be wilderness.

The sun is up now, and so is Gill. Traffic hums along the Hedge Road. The phone could ring at any minute. The rest of the world is setting about its business. I wish it a good day. It doesn't know, after all, what it's missing.

"SHELLEY SPEAKING"

SHELLEY AMBROSE, who works different hours than I do, starting later and staying long after I've gone home, stops every day on her way to the office and picks me up a large container of Irish-flavoured coffee. When she arrives, and before she even takes her coat off, she brings the coffee down to the control room, waits till there's a record or tape playing, and sidles into the studio taking the top off the coffee and leaving it near my right hand. Then she goes to her desk, fires up her computer and starts on her formidable daily tasks.

She begins usually with the clutter of letters I've left on top of her desk, which was neat when she left the evening before. On some of them I've scribbled terse instructions (she has deciphered samples of my handwriting that, a couple of hours after I've scrawled them, baffle even me). "Sorry," "Thanx," "Nice thanx," or "Tell him to blow it out his ear." Others call for as-kind-as-possible explanations of why we can't do an interview with someone's storied granduncle ("the first man to teach geometry to the Micmac"), originate *Morningside* from a bake sale in Swift Current, Saskatchewan, or send a pair of my used eyeglasses to be auctioned for a grade six excursion to Nepal.

Meanwhile, the phone starts ringing.

"Shelley speaking," she answers with unfailing good cheer and goes on to deal with callers who range from my bank manager, wondering if I know how much I'm overdrawn, to my kids asking if I was serious about supper Friday night. In between, various editors ask why my copy is late, listeners want to argue with what they're sure I said about turbans in the Mounties, someone needs to know the name of the Newfoundland fiddler who played what they think was a jig in the second hour (right after the lady author with the book about sparrows), Gill wonders if I paid the rent (she really means did Shelley write the cheque), the dentist reminds me of tomorrow's appointment, a weekly paper in British Columbia would like to reprint three letters from *The Morningside Papers* whose authors have long since disappeared, and a nice, elderly lady inquires if my sister went to St. Mildred's College in 1932. No, Shelley tells the last caller politely, that was Peter's aunt.

"Letters done?" I ask impatiently. (They are.) "And did I tell you someone called me at home last night and I've agreed to write an essay on the flag—see what there is in the library, will you?—and that I promised the people at Queen's you'd fax them that stuff on Meech Lake."

"Okay," she says still cheerily. "Do you want to have a golf meeting later on?"

I haven't even mentioned the golf. In 1990, the International Literacy Year, there will be seven golf tournaments in my name to raise money for that cause. They'll take place from Victoria to Fredericton, with one for good measure on the ice at Yellowknife, Northwest Territories, with sixteen people, all coordinated by Shelley—"and don't forget long underwear"—flying from various parts of the country for a couple of days of stories, songs, feasts and games. While all the tournaments, including the Arctic's, are run and supported by local committees, none of them could even tee off their first ball if it weren't for Shelley's energies, skills, patience or organizational abilities.

I don't know how she does it. I met her in 1987, when, fresh out of journalism school, she showed up at a bookstore where I was autographing one day. She was carrying her résumé, some sample clippings and—a signpost for the future—a container of coffee. Without being asked, she started opening copies of my book at the right page for signing, noting people's names so I could thank them for the small gifts they brought in and generally making herself useful.

Since then, she has turned herself into not only my correspondence coordinator and typist but my travel agent, business manager, gift buyer, appointment handler, anniversary reminder, tax consultant, conscience and friend. I could not get along without her.

There are, to be sure, a lot of aspects to her job that are more involving than those I've listed. She edits all the mail that gets on *Morningside,* for instance, and produces the segments that Shelagh Rogers and I read on the air, and on the book projects we work on together she is as much editor as typist and coordinator. But what impresses me most about her—aside from her unfailing good spirits—is that, in her mind, at least, there seems to be no separation between the most menial of work and the most intellectually stimulating. Nothing is beneath her.

She has, I know, a number of counterparts in the working world. A decreasing number are called secretaries, most preferring "assistant" or, more gloriously, "executive assistant." Shelley, who seems to know all of them, just talks about "so-and-so's me."

But I think we should realize how important they are, and what an encouraging signal they send about the future. In a time when those of us enjoying the best years of our lives often complain about the way young people don't seem to work as hard as we did, they are the exception. They deserve some celebration.

A Taste of Oenophilia

ᘓ

"But we'll be able to tell which are Canadian," said my friend Peter Sibbald Brown, wrinkling his nose. "They'll be the ones in the screw-top bottles."

Peter knew better, I'm sure. He is, as well as being one of this country's finest book designers, a pretty knowledgeable guy. Furthermore, I happen to know, he drinks Canadian wines from time to time. Still, this was a wine-tasting, and a little snobbery at the start—even false snobbery designed to draw a laugh—didn't seem out of place.

We had gathered partly because of the attitude Peter's tongue-in-cheek remark exemplified: that Canadian wines are mostly plonk, and if you put them up against *real* wines they'd never hold their own.

Truth is, I used to be guilty of that attitude myself. As a young husband, I would sometimes decant Brights Manor St. Davids, the only wine I could afford, into French bottles and pour it for my unsuspecting friends. But that was years ago, and almost since I could afford not to, I would no more have served Canadian wines in my home than I'd have offered fiddleheads from Georgia or snails (ugh) from my own back garden.

Almost, that is, but not quite. A couple of years ago, for reasons that still aren't clear to me, I started buying, drinking and serving (in their own bottles) Canadian wines. I liked them, but—well, I still wasn't sure.

Which is why, one day last autumn, I decided to hold the wine-tasting. Three couples took part: Peter S. B. and Marion Kilger; Martin O'Malley and Karen O'Reilly, the Cheery O's, as everyone calls them; and Gill Howard and I. Five of us, each now ready with paper and pencil, would do the tasting. Gill, who never drinks anyway, would supervise.

The tasters, I should point out, were not true connoisseurs. Though all of us *like* wine—Martin and Karen, in fact, spent a year in the Napa Valley of California, getting to know the vineyards and the wine world—none of us could be described, even if we could pronounce it, as oenophiles. But, as Martin said while we were settling in, the kind of tasting we were about to hold was often used by the wine makers themselves; they want to know what the experts think, but they're just as interested in the views of real people—their customers.

I had bought twelve wines, all chardonnays, one of the most popular whites of the nineties. Six were from Ontario (I had tried but been unable to get at least one British Columbia label); two came from California, and one each from France, Italy, Chile and Australia. They ranged in price from $7.00, which I'd paid for a Concha y

Toro from Chile, to $15.95, for one particular bottle of Ontario Hillebrand. The expensive Hillebrand was one of that company's premium chardonnays, which carry the vineyard's name on the label. The rest were more mid-range: $9.05 for the Australian (Lindeman's Bin 65); $7.95 and $10.75 for the Californians, and so on. The Canadians had about the same price spread as the imports, and, to be fair, I'd included not only a top-of-the-line Hillebrand but a mid-priced one—Barrel Aged 1989, at $11.95—and their chardonnay *ordinaire,* called Harvest, at $8.95.

I'd called some experts before we held our tasting and, following their instructions, we put the wines in the fridge exactly two hours before we started, to get them to the proper fifty degrees Fahrenheit. Now, as Gill removed and uncorked them, she wrapped each bottle in a liquor-store brown paper bag, numbered the bag and noted the number on her master list. Then, one by one, she brought them to the table.

As well as our pencils and papers, the table held extra glasses rented for the occasion (even though my experts had said you don't really need a clean glass for every sample of similar wines), some bread to cleanse our palates—no cheese, the experts had said; it affects the taste—and a bucket to (sigh) catch the leftovers after we'd sipped. Gill had outlawed spitting, which true oenophiles do. Too much like baseball, she said.

For the next hour or so, we had a wonderful time sampling the wines, recording our comments on colour, bouquet and taste and, individually, grading each anonymous wine on a scale of one to ten. When we were finished, we pooled our scores and our comments. Only after we'd ranked our choices did Gill reveal their identities.

For amateurs, we scored with remarkable consistency. The all-round winner was *everybody's* first choice; the least favourite was near the bottom of all lists, though it fell to last, I'm sure, because someone—I think it was Peter—gave it a zero. Universally, we found the Italian entry too thin, and admired the deep colour—though we didn't give high ratings to the taste—of the Australian.

Enough suspense.

The Canadians did *spectacularly* well. Our clear winner—we were quite proud of ourselves for having found it—was the premium Hillebrand. But in second place came the *lowest*-priced Hillebrand, the $8.95 Harvest, obviously, to our taste, the best buy. A Californian, from Ernest & Julio Gallo, was third, Canada's Cave Spring ($11.65) fourth, and tied for fifth and sixth were the Concha y Toro and—giving Canada four of the top six—Hillebrand's Barrel Aged. Somewhat to our surprise, for we all drink it from time to time, the Australian entry was well down the list.

Our least favourite? Let's grant it anonymity, shall we? It was Canadian, I blush to say. But no, Peter, it didn't have a screw top.

THE BEST BARBECUE COOK
IN THE HISTORY OF THE
WORLD

A JOKE I USED TO KNOW said that if you were planning a trip into the deepest wilderness you should pack a bottle of gin and a bottle of vermouth, and never open them unless and until you became hopelessly lost. Then, wherever you were, when you took your two bottles out of your kit bag, someone would come over the horizon and tell you how to make a better martini.

Nowadays, I think, when martinis are out of fashion anyway, you could substitute, for the gin and vermouth, a hibachi, some briquettes, matches and half a pound of sirloin. When you broke *them* out, no matter where you were, and before you could even open your matchbox, there'd be someone there—probably, in fact, your neighbour from the cottage—telling you you were starting your barbecue all wrong.

This is, I am convinced, the age when everyone is, or thinks he is, a champion at the grill. So the claim I am about to make is a bold and reckless one. But, what the heck, I'm a bold and reckless guy. I am the best barbecue cook in the history of the world, and it's time everyone else knew it.

Evidence? Well, for openers, I don't need a cookbook—even one as good as *Canadian Living*'s (though I do admit to picking up the odd useful hint therein, or lifting a few suggestions about salads and soups). Recipes are for the novice and the insecure. *I* just scout the fridge and cupboards, select my meat *du jour* as Van Gogh might have chosen his daffodils, ad lib the ingredients of my marinade—I wouldn't *dream* of measuring—and hit the golf course. Then, when the sun dips and my brew has steeped, I fire up the gas, stand back and, when the grill's hot, sizzle till done. The aromatic smoke curling over my cedar deck signals the arrival of gastronomic perfection as clearly as a puff of white over the Vatican hails the election of a new pope.

It's all done by instinct and natural genius. The closest I can come to capturing on paper the symphonic balance of one of my exquisite vegetable-kabob marinades, for instance, is: several generous tilts of the olive-oil bottle (I know you can get away with vegetable oils, but I am of the school that won't cook with wine you wouldn't drink, and happily drench my peppers and onions with golden extra-virgin); a healthy splash of bottled lemon juice (lime juice is an interesting variation); a spritz of red-wine vinegar—ah, go ahead, spritz it again; some soy sauce; a few knife-tops of *dry* mustard; as much commercially mashed garlic as you can scoop out of the jar with the handle of a spoon (anyone who minces his own garlic for a marinade is only showing off that he, too, knows how to pound it first with the side of a knife); a dash or two of Worseste—Worcheser—Worsechestersh—Lea & Perrins sauce; salt, pepper—*lots* of fresh ground black pepper; basil, thyme, rosemary, dill (dill's important), marjoram, oregano, dried parsley and whatever other leaves and stems smell good in your cupboard. And maybe a touch more of that wine vinegar. And, while you're at it, another grind of pepper.

Et voilà. Compare, for example, the recipe in *The Canadian Living Barbecue and Summer Foods Cookbook,* which calls for many of the same ingredients (though they miss the dill and the Worce—ah, forget it), but asks you, for heaven's sake, to measure out 2 mLs—what's an mL, anyway? it sounds like physics class—of your dried thyme.

I'm just as casual—casual but controlled, like Bill Evans at the piano—about the veggies themselves. Peppers are good, red and green and, in season, yellow. Don't bother to core them, just start slicing arcs off the sides. Scrape the biggest seeds off your slices and throw away what's left. Same with onions: peel, and cut chunks off the sides, about three layers thick, throwing away the square core. Mushroom caps give you the most delicate flavour on the kabobs, and soak up the marinade eagerly, but you have to buy the biggest mushrooms you can find, so they make discs as big as your pepper slices. Structurally, zucchini slices are a cinch, but after years of experimenting—and, yes, I've tried blanching them first—I agree with a guy who wrote a letter to the *Globe and Mail* and said that now that science had discovered that running an electric current through zucchinis made them explode, why didn't they just do that to all zucchinis everywhere, and blow them out of existence. Tomatoes? Eggplant? Sure, if you're in the mood. Even a chunk or two of squash. But my *coup de grâce* is a *tin* of *cooked* potatoes; the right size, the right consistency, wonderful absorbers of the marinade and, when you take them off the skewer, a tawny brown.

Potatoes, by the way, are the basis of my barbecue masterpiece: scalloped potatoes. I stole this idea from Bonnie Stern on the radio one day, but have so amended it after my own experimentation—oh, all right, with some consultation from Gill—that I think of it as my own. It's simplicity itself: sliced potatoes, skins and all, sliced onions (you peel *them*), salt, pepper, tablespoon-sized pieces of butter and slices—hunks, really—of Cheddar cheese, and maybe a sprinkling of oregano. Wrap the whole caboodle in foil. Before you seal it, make a kind of boat of the foil and pour in a pint or so of sinfully rich cream. Again, it's not the measurement that counts, it's the enthusiasm and the sure touch—food, especially around barbecues, *knows* when you're confident.

Other principles from my encyclopaedic knowledge: nuke your chicken or ribs in the microwave, wallowing in their sauces, before you put them on to brown (a little carbon never hurt you, by the way); you *can* clean a grill with foil, shiny side down, over the hottest flame you can muster for about half an hour; the best way to do steak is in one huge piece, sliced after you cook it (a good tip for checking on how well it's done, which I picked up from the poet Patrick Lane, is to cook a smaller piece on the side); a whole fish, painted with oil and stuffed with lemon and garlic and cooked in foil, may *in theory* be the same as if you'd done it in the oven, but in real life is *much* better barbecued—and much else that I could tell you if you wanted.

I'm sure you get the point, though. Now, if you'll just let me show you the right way to light that . . .

"And Long May Your Big Jib Draw"

ॐ

ACTUALLY, I HAD SEEN THE COD before dinner. One of the organizers had taken it to the prize table, where I was standing, sipping a rum. But, on the off chance the tales I'd heard were rumours, and not wanting to look like a greenhorn, I hadn't said anything.

The cod was dried, head missing, tail intact. It smelled—well, it smelled like a cod, not my idea of a turn-on. The tales, it was turning out, were true.

I was on my knees, in front of the head table. A man named Russell Fudge, as big as a linebacker in yellow fisherman's pants, rubber boots and cap, was holding the cod before me. Around the rest of the long tables that filled the atrium of a shopping mall, a couple of hundred happy Newfoundlanders chortled in anticipation. The ceremony was reaching its climax.

"And now," said Russell Fudge, "kiss the cod."

THOUGH I SPENT one university summer working in Labrador—iron ore, rushing rivers and the biggest and cruelest blackflies known to God—I didn't get to Newfoundland proper until 1971. I liked it from the beginning, and have since gone back as many times as I could. When my daughter, a CBC radio producer, had a chance to go to work there a couple of years ago, I urged her to accept. More than any other part of the country, I told her, Newfoundland is a place of its own, with its own long history, its own customs, its own geography, even, of course, it own colourful speech. You should get to know it before, as could happen one day in the Global Village, it, too, gets homogenized.

It's also much prettier than anyone who hasn't been there thinks. "The Rock," to use a name whose barren overtones bother some of its citizens, is in fact rich in landscape: reaching forests, teeming lakes, dramatic fiords. The first time I was in Cornerbrook, the metropolis of Newfoundland's under-appreciated west coast, I asked what the snow conditions were on the nearest ski slopes. "Just a moment," said my host. "I'll drive out and look." He was back in ten minutes.

Slowly, for Newfoundlanders are shy with the people they call Come-From-Aways—"it's as if you have to stay for a year before they realize you're here by choice," she said—my daughter fell in love with the place. She learned to walk the historic, hilly streets of St. John's in the gentle fog, to watch for icebergs at Pouch Cove (that's *Pooch* Cove to the uninitiated, just as Newfoundland is properly pronounced to rhyme with "understand"), to dine on caribou stew and pan-fried fish, to enjoy herself at parties. "If you go to a bar in Toronto," she reported once, "everyone sits around with a glum expression and drinks *seriously*. Here, they go for fun."

MY DAUGHTER WAS at least partially responsible for my kneeling in front of the cod.

Last year, the people who support Terra Nova National Park, the fingers of the sea that reach with aching loveliness into Newfoundland's eastern shoulder, were looking around for a guest "celebrity" for their fund-raising golf tournament. They called her, and, through her, me.

I played. The park's course, Twin Rivers, is a much better layout than I am a golfer—narrow, sloping fairways, cut from the boreal forest, with thickets of blueberries, or partridge berries as they call them in Newfoundland, deep in the evidence of passing moose. But, score notwithstanding (and we will let that astronomical number fade into history), I had a wonderful time. For all its difficulty, Twin Rivers presents some breathtaking scenery: a salmon river, its bank lined on opening day with anglers in hard hats, winds its way among the impossible fairways, and one hole, the eighth, is a single (you hope) four-iron over a postcard rugged gorge. No one, not even Twin Rivers' aptly named pro, Jim Stick, took the golf as seriously as the good fellowship. On the second of the tournament's two days, I was deep in clubhouse conversation with Newfoundland's still newly elected premier, Clyde Wells—just getting to

Meech Lake, I was—when I was summoned away by a mysterious telephone page, which turned out to have come from Stick, ensconced in his basement office and in need of one of the cold beers he had won from me the previous day.

In Newfoundland, I was reminded, first things first. The dinner with the cod ceremony was the climax of the event. After the golf, we all trooped over to Clarenville, where a banquet was spread on the long tables of the mall. When we had licked our plates clean of seafood casserole, lasagna, hip of beef, various greens and Black Forest cake, and when the prizes had been distributed—the only man to conquer Twin Rivers was rewarded with an Air Canada ticket to anywhere of his choosing (I'd have elected simply to come back the next year)—Russell Fudge, in his fisherman's gear and bearing a forty-ouncer of Newfoundland's nuclear-powered national drink, screech, along with the cod I had seen at the prize table, took centre stage.

"Down on your knucks," he commanded.

Quicker than I could look up knucks in *The Dictionary of Newfoundland English,* a copy of which had been presented to me at dinner, I dropped to my knees. I was, I knew from the tales, about to be "screeched in"—made an honorary citizen by dubious if well-meant ritual.

Fudge poured three fingers of screech, offered it to me, then drank it himself in one gulp.

"Repeat after me," he said. "Yes indeed me old cock I loves to be a screecher, and long may your big jib draw."

Somehow, perhaps because Fudge hadn't yet passed the screech, I repeated it.

Then he passed the screech. Then he held up the smelly grey cod and gave me my orders.

And then, my dears, I kissed it.

Knickknacks, Paperbacks, Photographs, Pins

∾

"Look," I say, "a match box from Tra Vigne, that restaurant in California where—"

"Out," says Gill.

"But don't you remember that dinner?" I say. "That's where we made Kevin and Sheila take us after—"

"Out," says Gill. "Along with your Yes and No buttons from the Fixed Link debate in Charlottetown."

"But some day they'll be—"

"Out," says Gill. "And while you're at it, pitch those programs from the Winnipeg Folk Festival and the four-year-old tin of seal meat from Newfoundland. We don't need the poster from the 1988 Trillium Book Award, either, the one with your name somewhere in the small type, or that toy car the CBC gave you when you were whining that someone in private radio got a Porsche as a signing bonus. And you can throw out that whole *box* of—"

THIS IS, as you have probably deduced, moving day at our apartment in Toronto. The day before, actually, a Friday. On Saturday, the professionals will come. Leaving us only the bare essentials to survive the weekend—coffee maker, cups, toothbrushes and half a bottle of Scotch—they'll pack our worldly goods into cartons. On Monday, they'll lug the boxes and our furniture out to the elevator and down to their van, drive them halfway across the city and lug them, again, up two flights of stairs into our bright new home.

The professionals—Larry, Curly and Moe, as I have come to call them—are an extravagance. I have only recently managed to talk Gill into hiring them. For weeks she has been determined to do all this on her own. (Are the drudgeries of moving the last of women's sole responsibilities, I wonder? Are women the only people decisive enough to handle this sort of thing?) But as the day has grown closer, and the sheer volume of the work involved more evident, she has at last relented to my pleas of both a bad back—I'd have to do *something*, after all—and a lack of willingness to watch her work.

All this week, though, we've been getting ready for Larry & Co. Which has meant, largely, doing what we're doing now: throwing out.

It's amazing, isn't it, what we accumulate? This is the fourth and last of the rooms we've had to strip for action. The other three have already yielded a cornucopia of superfluity. From the kitchen: jams, jellies and sticky syrups. Withered spices, hardened mustards. Extra lids, broken utensils. And Tupperware—where *does* it come from? Gewgaws and bric-à-brac from the living room. Clothes from the bedroom and the closets. My sons have carried off a wheelbarrowful of sweaters and jackets that used to fit me, a surprising number of which are now back in fashion, and one of my daughters will look, this spring, like an apprentice Gill. But other unwanted items have gone either to the Goodwill—at least one person down on his luck will get to wear a pseudo-velvet suit from my earliest television career—or, alas, just down the garbage chute. Four green garbage bags have tumbled to oblivion. From the kitchen alone, we've thrown out enough to stock a garage sale—or hold our own Tupperware party.

And coins. Everywhere we have looked there have been jars, bottles, cans of coins. Pennies, nickels, dimes, quarters, and, in one private Sierra Madre in my bedside drawer, six bright loonies. Is this a symptom of my undeserved prosperity? Maybe. There is enough unspent lucre in this apartment to buy cheeseburgers for half a class of hungry *kinder*. But I am, I know, not alone. In this age of inflated money, small change—most especially pennies—is more clutter than coinage. It chokes our purses and weighs down our trousers. We spill it onto our night tables and shove it to the backs of drawers. There are, I read somewhere, a *billion* pennies in Canadian houses—enough money to run *Morningside* for ten years. Maybe if we all moved every couple of years we could get it back into circulation.

Now, in the study—the second bedroom really, but given its ostentatious title because it's where I work (and collect, apparently)—we have hit the mother lode.

Knickknacks, paperbacks, photographs, pins. Costume jewels, broken tools, canisters, tins. Postcards, playing cards, business cards, tacks. Paper-clips, poker chips, model ships, wax. Two more garbage bags burst their seams.

Where, oh where, has it all come from? That chunk of rock, I know, is something one of my sons stuck in my Christmas stocking the year he'd been travelling in Europe. "Piece of the Berlin Wall," he said. But from the twinkle in his eye I knew that unless Teperman the wrecker had been working Germany, it was more likely domestic. The wind-up camel is a Christmas present, too—from Patsy, my boss, who thought it walked like me. And there are other gifts and presentations, some thoughtful (we'll keep them), some with their humour showing its age.

But mostly it's just—stuff. The stuff of our lives together, Gill's and mine, souvenirs of long-forgotten trips, mementoes of occasions lost to time. The new place is smaller, more efficient—and, of course, ours; we have rented these rooms for longer than we ever intended. It's a new start, a new chapter in our lives. Even the plants that Gill has nurtured here, making some corners of the apartment look like outposts of the Ecuadorian jungle, will go to friends, and she'll start anew in her own place.

Inevitably, I know, we'll accumulate again. Meantime, much of this has to go. And the truth is, if not for the enforced watershed of moving, we'd never have looked at it at all.

Still, tidying it up—throwing it out—is hard, a mixture of nostalgia and bemusement.

"Remember this?" says Gill. "It's the file you made of Anglicisms from the *Globe and Mail*'s cryptic crossword. You were going to write—"

"Out," I say. "Larry and Curly will be here tomorrow."

As Good a Man
as I Know

MAN, CAN TOM JACKSON SHOOT POOL!

I have known of his skills by reputation for a long time. But this, actually playing him, is something else again. We start with a simple game of straight pool. He asks if I want a handicap. Half in jest, I say, "Sure, six balls." (There are only seven a side.) "Okay," Tom says. Then he breaks, takes off six of my balls by hand, and, in one turn, shoots all seven of his own.

We try nine-ball, an easier game. It's still no contest. Every time he ambles up to the table and bends that long six-foot-five frame over his cue he's off on a long run—usually to the end of the game. He's *uncanny*. Click, amble, click, amble, click, click, click. And, like all great money players, he often seems to win by accident. "Oh, sorry," he says, and smiles as the shooter spins off the object ball and knocks in the nine for another win. "Want to try again?"

We are, thank heaven, playing for fun. I learned long

ago not to play *anything* with him for money. Veterans of the folk-music circuit still talk about one post-festival session in Edmonton in the seventies, when I tangled with him at gin rummy, a game I thought I understood. Let's just say I understood it better when we finished.

Tom Jackson is as good a man as I know. Not just good at games, but at . . . well, at being a good man. The CBC's *fifth estate* ran a profile of him last season, celebrating his remarkable acting achievements in *North of 60* and *Shining Time Station* on TV, in *The Diviners* on film (he *was* Jules Tonnerre), and in *Dry Lips Oughta Move to Kapuskasing* on the stage. He was, they said, "just about the busiest actor in Canada." Yet they called their piece, accurately, "Acting comes second."

It does, too—to feeding the hungry and housing the homeless. Years ago, well before his acting career took off, Tom started holding Christmas concerts in Winnipeg, where he lives (he was born in Alberta, but moved to Winnipeg as a teenager), to raise money for food. The concerts are named after the Huron Carol, which he sings in his rich and powerful bass—he was a singer long before he discovered acting—and there's a tape called the Huron Carol, all the proceeds of which go to the Salvation Army. The concerts have spread. There's one in Calgary now, which he set up when they were shooting *North of 60* in southern Alberta, and tapes of it for sale. And so on and so on. But that's only part of it. Tom works nearly all the time, hustling money for good works the way he used to hustle at the pool table. That's what matters to him; the singing and the acting just pay his bills.

He knows what it's like to be down and out. I remember flying out to Winnipeg once, to lend him a hand with the Huron Carol. He met me at the airport, on a searingly cold December day. On the way downtown, I asked him about the people he was raising the money for. "I've never figured how people could live on the streets in this kind of winter," I said. "Where do they *sleep,* for heaven's sake?"

"Oh, you learn," Tom said. "Did you see that Indian kid we passed a few blocks ago—the tall guy with the jeans jacket and his hands stuffed into his back pockets? That was me, once. You just survive, that's all. You get to know where the warm doorways are. You learn which buildings leave their lobbies open, and how to move up and down the stairwells against the rhythm of the security guy. You learn."

I don't know what turned his life around. It's like the racism he suffered as a kid—he never talks about it. (The most powerful sequence in the *fifth estate* profile comes when Trish Wood, the reporter, asks him about being a half-English half-Cree kid in a white environment, and Tom just stares her down in that deep, still way he has, before he says, "Everyone says you expose the poison to find the cure. But the poison's *been* exposed a thousand times. Now let's just find the cure.")

In twenty years of friendship, in fact, the only time I've ever really heard him talk about himself has come today, the afternoon of our pool game. We're in Inuvik, high on the Mackenzie Delta, on one of my annual adventures in playing golf on the ice for literacy. We've spent the afternoon in the schools. (The pool game is just a way to kill time till the plane takes us south again.) Tom's been busy. At the elementary school, he broke out his guitar and went minstrelling among the kids squatted on the gym floor. In the high school library, he kept some of the toughest kids in the North spellbound for two hours. There, he talked frankly and honestly, in language the young people could understand, about his own tempestuous youth. He'd been lucky, he said. He still couldn't write very well. Without the happenstance of his beautiful voice, who knows where he'd have ended up?

When he finished, they lined up for his autograph— *North of 60* is hugely popular north of sixty. A lot of the kids presented their jackets to be signed. He scribbled on the arms. Sometimes, he had to ask two or three times how to spell a name. But when he signed those sleeves, someone said, it was if he was inoculating the kids against dropping out.

Good thing, too. They'd never be as good as he is at the pool table.

No One but Fools
or Weaklings
—or Me

ॐ

In yellowknife, a year or so ago, I fell into conversation with a pair of German tourists.

"So how do you like our northern capital?" I asked.

"Very nice," they replied. "Except for all the prostitutes."

"Prostitutes?" I said. "In *Yellowknife*?"

"Sure. All those women lining the streets, smoking cigarettes and—"

I understood. Yellowknife is a civil service town. A few days before our conversation, the Northwest Territories government had banned smoking in all its buildings. The women the tourists had seen braving the Arctic chill were just grabbing a few puffs of poisoned fumes before they attacked the next stack of memos.

It's happening everywhere. Yellowknife, on the frontier (though you can get good greens there now, trucked in overnight from Edmonton, and there's a chocolate boutique in the mall), is only the latest Canadian capital to outlaw smoking on publicly owned premises. And government buildings are not alone. You can't light up *anywhere* indoors now, even, for heaven's sake, in the Skydome in Toronto. The erosion—erosion, hell, demolition—of the right to smoke around other people is the most evident social change of the past decade. It has reshaped not only the way we live together—smokers, I can attest, now think twice about whose house they'll go to for dinner, just as non-smokers are choosy about whom they'll kiss—and how the places we inhabit smell, but how they look. The ugliest side effects of the new age, surely, are the piles of half-smoked butts that litter the doorways of public buildings. The saddest are the crowds of people outside hospitals, dragging their ivs behind them, with their bare bums flapping from their gowns, puffing away on yet another sample of what, in all likelihood, laid them low in the first place. When I was a kid, no self-respecting woman would think of smoking on the street; now, since that's often the *only* place she can do it, you see it all the time.

When I was a kid—ah, me. I wonder if the people who take such relish in condemning smokers—the smoke Nazis, as my friend Catherine Ford of the Calgary *Herald* calls them—realize how hard we worked to get started, coughing and spluttering over every stolen Sweet Caporal, turning green and dizzy as we learned to inhale, fighting our nausea until, at last, we could drag without expiring.

Smoking was smart a generation ago. Cool. (Remember Kools, with menthol to hide the taste of tar?)

Everyone did it. We saved our allowances for small packs of Turrets or larger ones of Buckinghams or Sportsmans. (Remember Sportsmans, with the fishing lures on the yellow package?) When we were flush we bought flat fifties—pale blue for Winchesters, forest green for Export "A"s, which had (remember this?) cork tips. Responding to the advertising that burbled from the radio and filled the magazines, we reached for an Old Gold ("not a cough in a carload") or a Lucky Strike (everyone my age knew what LSMFT meant, and some of us had naughty variations) or walked a mile for a Camel. To be adventurous (or when we were broke), we rolled our own; in those days cigarette papers were for cigarettes. Our parents smoked, our teachers smoked, our heroes smoked—in movies (we tried to droop our cigarettes from our mouths like Humphrey Bogart) and, later, like Edward R. Murrow, on television.

And now who smokes? According to the best figures I can dig up, twenty-seven per cent of all Canadians do—including babies, doctors and people in comas. That's down from forty-four per cent in 1966, but it still seems high to me. According to my own observations, *no one* smokes any more—or no one but fools, weaklings or that combination of both, me. My teeth are yellow, my fingers brown; my clothes stink and so, I'm sure, does my breath. There are holes in my rugs and scars on my furniture, and my computer keyboard is choked with ashes. Once, shielding a smouldering butt from the wind, I set fire to the pocket of my favourite windbreaker. More than once, holding a phone too near my ear, I've sniffed the acrid odour of sizzling hair. I haven't smoked in a radio studio in more than a year—those long records you hear on *Morningside* sometimes cover my frantic dash to the smoking room—but in my own office, as well as most of my friends' houses, I'm a pariah. I hate my habit, but somehow, remembering the price I paid to pick it up, I soldier on.

Yet even I am growing weary. Not converted, just weary. Smoking in the 1990s is almost more trouble than it's worth. You can't just do it any more; you have to go someplace—usually, if the buildings I work in around the country are any indication, into the sourest, grimiest, most airless rooms anyone can find. In most smoking rooms, you don't even have to light up to get your fix; you just breathe for a moment or two—or try to. At airports, smokers gather like lepers under the "designated" signs, desperately sucking up enough nicotine to last them across two time zones. (A friend called me a couple of months ago to say that if I absolutely had to get from Toronto to Vancouver—five hours of forced withdrawal on a Canadian airline—I should fly Air Thailand to Seattle, and hitchhike the rest of the way.) At dinner parties, when we do go, after gazing despondently around for ashtrays we gather on the back porch, huddling together against the cold. In taxis (not all of whose non-smoking drivers have the grace to put signs in their windows warning you of their zeal) we drum our fingers and ask, "How much longer till we get downtown?" And movies—remember "smoking loges"?—get longer all the time.

So why not quit? Oh, I will, I will—if I live long enough. But right now, I'm just stubborn enough to resist being legislated into good health. The bigger they put those warnings on the packages—does anyone think they're *news* to us?—the more perverse pleasure I take in defying them. I'm a different person than when I was a kid, much less interested in conforming and not, frankly, willing to work as hard to stop as I did to start.

Besides, when I do quit, where will I meet all those other fools, weaklings and government office workers? And, if we do meet, what will we have to talk about?

A Mushroom of
the Electronic Age

~

I BEGAN TO COME TO PEACE with the machines in my life at 11:06 A.M. on a Tuesday, last summer.

I was at our place in the country. I know it was a Tuesday because I had just finished one of these columns—the one on potatoes, if that matters—and it had been due, as usual, on the Monday.

I know it was 11:06 because there is a digital clock in the upper corner of my computer screen. You could see it now if you were looking over my shoulder. If you looked *past* the digital clock, up over the top of the computer and out through the louvred window, you could see the first fairway of the golf course where I play, which was where I had been looking when I took the first step toward my new relationship . . .

MACHINES, with their dials and buttons, their glowing numbers and their blinking LED displays, are everywhere in my life. I get up in the morning to the gentle beeping—it grows less gentle the longer you ignore it—of a two-alarm clock. (The other alarm will wake Gill later.) I defuse the electronic burglar alarm before I open the door for the morning paper, grind some coffee beans in a mill whose sound reminds me of the dentist's, and spoon the resulting blend into an automatic coffee maker. While the coffee brews, I turn on the television—by remote control—to see who won last night's hockey games or whether there's been an earthquake in Peru.

Even as the day begins, my incompatibility with machines shows through. More than once I have turned off Gill's alarm when mine rings, leaving her to snooze past the morning's first appointments. A lot more than once I have failed to close the receiving drawer at the bottom of the coffee mill, and spewed powdery grounds over half the kitchen (my little grinder has the force of a CF-18), or neglected to place the carafe in the coffee maker so that, while I've worked happily away on the cryptic crossword, piping hot coffee has cascaded over the naked hot plate, steaming and slurping to the floor.

All the machines in my life are smarter than I am—when they choose to be. My coffee maker, for instance, is quite capable of brewing me a cup while I sleep. But when I try to tell it to do that, it either does its work twelve hours too early (one of us can't tell A.M. from P.M.), greeting me with tepid sludge in the pre-dawn gloom, or just sits there full of cold water. If I could figure out how to program it, my VCR could trap the hockey scores after I've gone to bed and show them to me fresh when I awake. But I am no more capable of setting my recorder to record what I want than I am of playing "Bumble Boogie" on the harpsichord; whatever I ask for, it seems to prefer *The Newlywed Game,* or its own inventive mixture of white noise and commercials. The only part of VCR technology I have mastered is learning how to cover up, with electrical tape, the infernally blinking LED display with which it signals the passing of a power failure.

Power failures. I live in fear of them. Without a plastic card, I cannot escape the parking garage in my apartment building in Toronto, and I approach the thick steel automatic door each morning in dread of being locked forever in the basement, a mushroom of the electronic age. Once, as I typed furiously through a country thunderstorm, lightning blew two chapters off my computer's memory. (I hit SAVE every two paragraphs now, even when it isn't raining.) When the cable television turned to hiss one weekend, I spent $42.50 for service calls before I learned that the whole neighbourhood had been cut off by a fallen tree.

Even without the help of nature, machines confound me. The same computer that succumbed to lightning once, for no apparent reason, elected a pope while I was working—or so it appeared, since a puff of white smoke emerged from the back of the monitor. I have filled the dishwasher with laundry detergent, producing the frothy equivalent of magic porridge, exploded an egg and turned sausages to India rubber in the microwave and, by cramming too many tomatoes into the food-processor, decorated the kitchen with half-made, garlicky gazpacho.

At lot of this, I know, is just ineptitude. Things don't work for me. I'm no good with them. I have owned and driven the same car for nine years now, thanks to the genius of a good mechanic, but I learned only last spring—Gill told me—that there's a tool kit in the trunk. My idea of playing Mr. Fix-It around the house is changing the tank on the propane barbecue. But some of it has been deliberate, too. I don't *like* machines. I prefer people. I've never met a bank machine I could pass the time of day with, even the ones—have you *seen* these?—that call you by name when you punch your number in. I can't ask a video machine how it liked *Perfectly Normal,* or inquire about the weather in Saskatoon when a sexless computer gives me the number I seek. (Am I the only person who *thanks* that mechanical voice?)

ANYWAY, TUESDAY, 11:06 A.M. I have finished—at last—my potato column. As always when I work in the country, I have turned to yet another of the machines in my life, and faxed my copy to my ever-patient editor. The fax is a wonderful convenience, of course—it's minutes between when I finish printing the column out (if I can line up the holes in paper with the proper sprockets) and when it reaches Bonnie's desk. But it's yet another way personal contact is giving way to technology; in the old days, I'd have handed my copy to Bonnie and we'd have gone for a coffee when she'd read it. Today, the silence is oppressive. I want out of here. Outside the louvred window, the golf course beckons.

And then I think: Not many miles down the road, my

friend Martin O'Malley is also staring at a screen. Though Martin is often as tempted by golf as I am, I hesitate to call him because, like any writer, he resents the intrusive ringing of the phone when he works. But, I realize, he has just had a fax machine installed.

I fire up the computer once more—this is how I know the time. I type out as seductive a message as I can about the pleasures of golf and my willingness to wager on my own laughable abilities, and slip it into the fax. I dial O'Malley's number and punch SEND. My message will not interrupt him, I know, but if he feels like playing hookey for the afternoon . . .

Moments later—there is still no sound—the word comes back, slipping smoothly out of the machine. "You're on," O'Malley has replied, and typed out the conditions of the bet *he* is prepared to make. I smile in anticipation. Heaven bless technology, I think as I go to look for my golf shoes.

CANADIAN STUDIES

~

In THE SUMMER OF 1964, for reasons unimportant here, I left my job at *Maclean's* magazine, where I had worked for six years.

The best of those years, for me at least, I had spent in Quebec, where I had written about what we all called the "Quiet Revolution"—a phrase I used so often in *Maclean's* that a lot of people thought I'd coined it. I had been moved by what I saw there. I felt that unless the rest of us figured out how to respond to the forces I had seen unleashed, the country I had grown up in would have a hard time holding together. But I also felt the rest of us *were* responding, or trying to, and I was as frustrated by Quebec's inability—or unwillingness—to see that as I was at the anglophone ignorance of Quebec.

I was thirty years old. Like everyone else of that age and time, I was, as we said, into folk music. I knew all the verses (though not necessarily in the right order) of

"Tambourine Man" and even the guitar chords—C, D⁷, G, if you want proof—for "If I Had A Hammer."

I also knew Ian and Sylvia. I had met Sylvia in Chatham, Ontario, when I was a young newspaperman and she was the choir-mistress's teenage daughter, and I had followed her career as she joined up with and eventually married Ian Tyson to form the pre-eminent couple of Canadian folk.

One evening, the three of us were talking about where songs come from. I asked Ian, who had already written the magical "Four Strong Winds," if he thought the well would ever run dry.

"Not for melodies," he said. "But I'm sometimes short of ideas for lyrics."

"If I could write music . . ." I said, and a beer or two later, Ian was picking out one of his spare tunes for me on the guitar. Over the next few days, I set some words to it, a kind of folk condensation of some of what lingered from my time in Quebec.

In my lyrics, a man (presumably) addresses a woman. (It could be the other way round.) "How come we can't talk to each other any more," says the singer. "Why can't you see I'm changing, too?" The chorus, a lament for the way things were, begins, "One single river rolling onward to the sea," and ends, "but just one river rolling free."

Pretty melancholy stuff. But heartfelt.

I wish I could report that "Song for Canada"—as we called it in case anyone missed the point—was an instant hit. Instead, the opposite was true. Our song made its

debut at Massey Hall in Toronto. For some reason—
maybe because Ian introduced it as "a little something the
journalist Pete Gzowski and I have written" or maybe
because my lyrics emphasized the pseudo-Oklahoma
twang that even folksingers from Ontario affected in
those days ("Haow come we cain't . . .")—the audience
thought we were trying to be funny. Before they figured
out that we weren't, they were giggling. I wanted to disappear under my seat cushion

Later on, the Chad Mitchell Trio recorded "Song for
Canada," someone translated it into French, and someone else included Ian's melody in "Nine Easy Songs for
the Five-String Banjo." I made, in fact, about a thousand
dollars. But other than that, and except for the occasional
grizzled folkie who remembers more of my lyrics than I
do now, my song-writing career is long over.

I'VE BEEN THINKING about "Song for Canada" in the
past few months.

I turned on the television to watch the St. Jean Baptiste
Day celebrations in Quebec, just after the failure of
Meech Lake. On Ile Ste-Hélène in Montreal, I saw a
hundred thousand Québécois, many waving blue
fleurs-de-lis, gathered for a concert of five major stars:
Gilles Vigneault, Paul Piche, Michel Rivard, Diane
Dufresne and Laurence Jalbent. At one point, Rivard,
who is balding and resembles a pop star about as much as I
do a tennis pro, strummed some introductory bars and
held the mike up to the audience. A hundred thousand

voices, or so it seemed, broke into the lilting words to his *"Je voudrais voir la mer,"* scarcely a "Song for Quebec" (Vigneault's *"Les Gens du Pays"* would fill that function better) but an anthem, nevertheless, a song *of* Quebec, an expression of the people and, I could not help thinking, unknown outside its borders. It was a long way from Massey Hall.

Any one of the stars at Ile Ste-Hélène, I reflected, could have filled Place des Arts for days if not weeks, and there are magazines that thrive simply by writing about their lives. Yet with the possible exception of Vigneault, whose lyrics transcend translation, all of them could walk down any main street in other parts of Canada without drawing a second glance. Every week on Quebec television, some two and a half million people tune in to a *téléroman*—a kind of prime-time soap opera—whose plot and stars are part of the weave of Quebec life, yet the rest of us don't even know it exists.

But if our knowledge of Quebec leaves something to be desired, they don't know us, either.

On the program I host on CBC Radio, Timothy Findley and some other literate Canadians were mourning the death of Margaret Laurence. Nathalie Petrowski, a brilliant young writer who covered cultural matters for *Le Devoir,* stopped everyone by saying she didn't know who Margaret Laurence was. There is not a single correspondent for the Quebec media stationed west of the Ottawa River, not a single chair of "Canadian" studies at a Quebec university, so all the dramatic changes that have occurred over the past generation in what the Québécois persist in calling *"Canada anglais"*—our own Quiet Revolution—have gone unnoticed in Quebec.

And so on and so on. Twenty-six years after Ian played me his melody, the mournful words of our now-forgotten song seem to apply as much as ever.

I wonder, now, if anyone would laugh.

AND THE BEST DAMN
STEW-MAKER TOO

ONE OF THE NICEST THINGS about growing up is the way you can enjoy all the foods you turned your nose up at as a kid.

Take liver. When I was young, liver was right up there with bullies and social studies on my list of things to be avoided. I still don't like bullies, and social studies, though I make a lot of my living talking about them on the radio, still give me trouble. (I miss all the blue questions at Trivial Pursuit, too.) But on liver I've come all the way round. From a pet hate it's turned into a favoured food; I eat it now—I would never have believed this when I was six—by choice, and lick my lips when I'm finished.

The liver I ate as a child, of course, was cut in slabs as thick as beaverboard and cooked till you could fix your roof with it. Now, I buy my slices as thin as I can—a quarter inch is about right—and eat it as rare as filet mignon. To cook it, I fry up some bacon first, and while it's sizzling I cut up a couple of onions. When the bacon's done, I set it aside on a paper towel, turn the heat down and sauté the onions in the drippings. When the onions are soft but not translucent, I set them aside, too, crank the heat back up, splash some wine vinegar into the pan ("deglazing" is too fancy a word for the way I cook) and sear my liver on each side for less time than it took Northern Dancer to win the Kentucky Derby—two minutes flat. Smothered in the bacon and onions, and with a little watercress vinaigrette on the side, it's food for the gods—or a grown-up.

Or spinach. Spinach was *punishment* when I was a kid: a soggy, mossy blob that lay on your plate like a mud pie, leaking green effluvium.

The trick with spinach, I know, is to cook it as little as possible. Just grab a handful, chop off the heaviest stems, run cold water over what you have left and, without shaking it dry, pop it into a saucepan, jam the lid on and cook on high for *one minute*—Northern Dancer's time for five furlongs. Want to get fancy? Squeeze half a lemon over the spinach before you start to steam it. Want to get *really* fancy? Plop a dob of sour cream on top as you bring your spinach to the table. With either or neither or both, it's wonderful.

This side dish, come to think of it, could go with your liver-and-bacon-and-onions, even though, if my mother found out I was recommending liver and spinach in one meal, she'd push her halo aside and scratch her head in wonderment.

THE GREATEST TREAT of all among the foods I once disdained is stew.

Stew was my mother's admission she'd run out of either ideas or money, a kind of dinner-hour equivalent of—and about as tasty as—the Red River Cereal she tried to convince me to eat in the mornings.

For the grown-up me, stew has become a source of sheer pleasure. I like eating it, spearing the tenderest cubes of nut-brown meat, savouring the gay orange carrots and pale parsnips—*parsnips?* my mother's halo just clattered to heaven's floor—and sopping up the last rivulets of dark gravy with chunks of fresh bread. I *love* cooking it, and in the long cold winter there is no happier way for me to spend a late Friday afternoon than to follow the ritual I am pleased to share with you now. The quantities, I should tell you, are for two people, though there'll be enough extra if someone drops in or, failing that, for a reheated (and delicious) Saturday lunch.

At the liquor store, get a bottle of dark, fairly dry sherry. Make sure they put it in a brown paper bag. (This may not help your reputation in a strange town, but be brave.)

At the butcher's, get a pound and a quarter of lean stewing beef, cut into inch-and-a-half cubes.

At the grocer's, pick up some leeks, cooking onions, a few carrots and parsnips, a tin of beef stock, a nineteen-ounce tin of tomatoes and a tin of whole, peeled potatoes. From a guy who likes things simple and old-fashioned, I know, this last suggestion will surprise you. But experience has taught me that even the best potatoes, cooked from scratch in a stew, get just a bit starchier than those little ones they put in the cans.

If you don't have butter, olive oil, flour, pepper (beef stews need no salt), garlic and other spices at home, pick those up, too. Oh, what the heck, get another couple of heads of garlic anyway.

And from your favourite bakery, get a fresh baguette.

If you have a fireplace, begin by lighting a fire to take the chill from the fading day. Then open your sherry and pour yourself a small glass—the shopping was cold, after all. Put a sinfully thick slice of butter and about a quarter cup of your best olive oil into a generously sized saucepan or soup kettle, and turn the heat to medium-high. While the butter melts and blends with the golden oil, take the paper bag from the booze store, put a cup of flour into it and grind some pepper on top. Throw the cubes of meat in the bag and shake it vigorously. Pick the meat out by hand—the way the flour coats every piece evenly is surely one of the great miracles of the kitchen—and put it in the pan. As it browns, chop three or four peeled onions into eighths, and the white parts of the same number of leeks into inches. Chop a *lot* of garlic—I use about five cloves, but you can never have too much—and scrape everything in with the meat. Reduce the heat, have a sip of sherry and take a moment to enjoy the seductive smell rising from the pan. Stir from time to time with a wooden spoon.

When the meat is brown, splash in about a cup—who measures?—of the sherry and the tin of beef stock. Add a sprinkle of oregano, if it pleases you, or a bit of sweet basil. Lower the heat a notch (you don't want to *boil* it), and savour the smell again as you open the tin of tomatoes.

This is a good time to cut up the carrots and parsnips, as well—I peel the parsnips but just scrape the roughest skin off the carrots. Try to get all your pieces roughly the size of Brazil nuts.

You can slow down now, while your stew simmers. In another twenty minutes or so, add the tomatoes, liquid and all, and root veggies, and, half an hour after that, the tinned potatoes. Give it another ten or fifteen minutes— there's no rush, you know—while you put out some bowls, forks and spoons. You can rip up the baguette by hand.

The result, like youth itself, would be wasted on kids anyway.

COLD COMFORT

AUDREY CHUBB OF EDMONTON caught my attention in the mail this spring with a note about a stew recipe. Enclosed with her appreciation was the page of *Canadian Living* on which my recipe had been printed. It was stained with telltale marks of my ingredients, a gravy mark here, a splash of sherry there—evidence, surely, of the love and enthusiasm that had gone into her own preparation.

Audrey Chubb, I realized as I dashed off a thank-you note, is my kind of cook, happily abandoned in her work, and I thought of her again when I began researching the subject of this little excursion into culinary pleasures: cold soups—or, as the cookbooks call them, with their index-ing pinkies raised on high, *chilled* soups.

For one thing, page 87 of my copy of *The Harrowsmith Cookbook*—the page with Joan Stevens's Cold Avocado Soup and Carol Frost's Chilled (there they go again) Zucchini Soup—looks remarkably like the *Canadian*

Living page Audrey sent to me. Near the bottom right-hand corner is a speck of what can only be zucchini skin (summer of '87, I'd guess), and higher up, like beige Rorschach blobs, are smatterings of the basis of so many of the soups I've concocted over the years, chicken stock.

For another, cold soups are, surely, the stews of summer: simple to make, rewarding to eat, therapeutic in their process.

Simple? Absolutely. Even vichyssoise, the grandmother of them all (it was invented at the Ritz Carlton in New York in 1917), is easier to make than to spell—and *far* easier to make than to say; it's "vichy-swahz," dammit, and the people who drop the final "s" hit the same clanger of false pretension as those who say "between you and I." All you do is gently fry some leeks and onions in butter till they're wilted, add some peeled, diced potatoes (and garlic if you're adventurous) and cook for about five minutes, pour in about four cups of chicken stock brought to life by lemon juice, and go for a walk while it simmers. Half an hour later, take the mixture off the stove and let it cool enough to work with. Then purée it in batches through the food processor and put it back in the pot with about the same amount of half milk and half whipping cream. Heat it through till the textures and flavours combine, then take it off and chill it for a couple of hours. Serve in cups or bowls, with some fresh chives scissored over the surface and lots of ground black pepper.

If you can do that, I'd argue—and who can't, eh, Audrey?—you're well on your way to a cornucopia of summer delights that run, like page 87 of my Harrow-smith cookbook, from one end of the alphabet to the other.

Rewarding? Except perhaps for the perfect salad, I can think of no product of the summer kitchen that pays back so little effort with so much lip-smacking enjoyment from the guests: "Maybe I'll just have *half* a second bowl while you put the steaks on," I can hear them saying even now.

For a little more adventure (if you haven't done this before), you might try a cold cauliflower soup. Once again, start by gently sautéing some onion in butter—*lots* of butter, maybe half a cup for one chopped onion. This time, instead of the leeks, and before you mix in the cauliflower, add a stalk or two of celery, also chopped. As it burbles—even in the heat of summer, there are few more appetizing smells—sprinkle a couple of tablespoons of flour over the top, and for some zest, a teaspoonful of curry powder and two drops of your favourite hot sauce.

Now the chicken stock. Truly serious cooks, I suppose—the tomato peelers—will have made their own, but I (and I'll bet Audrey Chubb, too) settle for the powdered version you can buy at a bulk-food store, with flecks of green herbs. I double the recommended intensity, mixing about two heaping tablespoons (I don't really measure) into a quart of hot water. Whichever, add about four cups to the simmering vegetables and cook slowly till everything's soft. As with the vichyssoise—and this is where, I confess, my cookbooks get stained—put everything through the food processor in batches (the big chopping blade does fine), and return to the pot. Add the yolk of an egg, salt and pepper and about a cup and a half of cream (I use whipping cream but my waistline shows it). Heat just enough to mix, then put it in the fridge. If company's on its way, stick it in the freezer for half an hour or so. For the chives this time, substitute sprigs of parsley.

ALL THESE CREAMY SOUPS—and the variety of vegetables you can build them from is only limited by your imagination (try asparagus some time, or the *Canadian Living Barbecue Cookbook*'s fresh pea and lettuce)—are, as I say, relaxing to make. But for true therapeutic value, I prescribe a handmade gazpacho.

There are, of course, as many recipes for gazpacho as there are (here's another cooling thought for summer) Inuit words for snow. More and more of them, in these technological times, use the food processor—as even I do for my variations on the theme of chicken stock and cream. But for sheer *satisfaction*—not to mention one of the great taste experiences of summer—try this:

Chop three big, juicy tomatoes, seeds, peel and all; three cucumbers, peeled and halved so you can scoop out the seeds with the tip of a spoon; three cored green peppers; five (even more, if you have the nerve) peeled cloves of garlic; and two giant peeled onions. Mix them all up in a big metal bowl.

Now add two cans of beef stock, two cans of water, a can of tomato juice, the juice of three lemons, salt, pepper and lots of fresh basil. Stir thoroughly with a big wooden spoon. On top of everything put some thin slices of onion, punched into rings, and some slices of peeled lemon. Cover it all—you don't want everything in the fridge to smell of garlic—and chill it overnight. Next day, serve it with a dollop of sour cream on top of every bowl.

Got that, Audrey?

Oh, by the way, if you sent me your copy of the stew recipe, how are you going to make it again?

CHILD OF THE LAND

WHEN ANN HANSON—Ann Meekitjuk Hanson, as she sometimes calls herself—was a girl, she was simply Annie E7-121, the daughter of a nomad couple. Her father, a hunter, died when she was three or four (she is not sure). Her mother, who taught her the traditional skills of her people, developed tuberculosis a few years later and was taken south, to Hamilton, Ontario, where, after a long and debilitating illness, she died.

Ann was a child of the land. She learned to fish, to sew parkas, to skin seals. In winter, she travelled by dog team, as her people had travelled from camp to camp for thousands of years. She knew when the first berries would show through the thinning ice, and where the ptarmigan hid. She could tell the difference, as she once wrote in a letter, between the sounds of silence in the winter—there were times in the winters of her childhood when all there was to put in her belly was hot water—and the sounds of silence in the spring. She spoke and thought in her native

Inuktitut. When she first went to school, at eight, she needed an interpreter.

The E that preceded her number stood not for Eskimo, as some people think, but for Eastern, though the figures themselves, which the children often wore around their necks like dog tags, were known as Eskimo numbers. In the western Arctic, the letter was a w. The first digit designated a zone. Annie E7-121 came from near Lake Harbour, on Baffin Island.

Ann Hanson is forty-three now, a smart, articulate, attractive wife and mother (her husband is one of the most important businessmen in Iqaluit), as comfortable in English, which she speaks with a northern lilt, as in her mother tongue. The years since her number was replaced by a name—the government finally ended the old system as a centennial project—have been eventful for her. After her mother died, she was adopted by an aunt who married a southerner and took Annie to Toronto for company. When she returned home, she recalls now, she was showing signs of "being bad." She envied southern women, with their lipstick and curly hair. Her people sent her south again. The rebellion disappeared, but not the determination to make something of herself. In Toronto, she studied at Shaw Business College, and became a secretary to the federal MP Gene Rhéaume. When Rhéaume was defeated she found herself stranded in Edmonton but, undaunted, she went home and signed on at the Northern Service of the CBC, where she rose quickly from receptionist to host of her own program, broadcasting in Inuktitut and working as an interpreter. When movie makers came from the south to make a film of James Houston's marvellous and authentic novel *The White Dawn,* which is set on Baffin Island in the days of the first white whalers—days Ann Hanson's grandparents might well have remembered—and, in spite of having auditioned almost every brunette actress in Hollywood, were unable to find anyone who looked the part of the Inuk heroine, they hired Ann. She came close to stealing the show. Movie acting mastered, she has since directed some television, continued to broadcast, to travel, to work as an interpreter and to raise her family.

Two years ago, Ann Hanson was appointed deputy commissioner of the Northwest Territories—the commissioner himself is a kind of lieutenant governor, whose powers, once autocratic, have gradually been turned over to the NWT's elected government—and last year, in that capacity, she had the duty of proroguing the house. On that occasion, the woman who had been Annie E7-121 spoke in Inuktitut. Although she was not the first native to be deputy commissioner of the NWT—Agnes Semmler from Inuvik held the post before her—she was the first person to speak her language from the speaker's chair, where she represented the authority of the Queen, and while, as she said, it took her "a long, long time to get unnervous," she was very proud of herself for that.

I HAVE JUST RETURNED from the North as I write. The trip was only my eighth or ninth into the Arctic since I first started going there in the early 1970s; I have not become what I have heard northerners call "a southern Inuk" as yet (nor what they call "an expert," which I once heard defined as some bastard from the south, with slides). But, as all my other trips have done, it made a powerful impact on me. Once again, I was overwhelmed by the majesty of the landscape, touched by the warmth of the people and dismayed at how left out they feel by the rest of the country. A thesis I sometimes toy with, in fact, is that the North is to the rest of us exactly what the rest of us are to the United States. It is more complex than the rest of us realize, much more interesting and pretty well ignored—most of the tourists I saw setting off for hiking trips into the achingly beautiful mountains, cliffs and glacial lakes of Auyuittuq National Park were Europeans.

The North is also changing faster than any other part of Canada. Far too much authority is still exercised by Ottawa and other southern centres, but nearly every month, it seems, the legislative assembly in Yellowknife assumes more power over its own region's destiny. And the majority of the members of that assembly, I remind you—whose dealings the former minister of northern affairs David Crombie has called the most interesting political process in the western world—are now native.

The changes, and the stresses that accompany them, are taking their toll. As just one sign, on Baffin Island alone, where the total population is about the same as that of Yarmouth, Nova Scotia, more than one hundred people, mostly young males, have committed suicide in the past ten years—an epidemic that, if it had occurred in Yarmouth, would have been a scandal of international dimensions.

But there are other aspects of the changes, too, and the story of Ann Hanson, the deputy commissioner—Annie E7-121—is one of them.

None for Us, Thanks, There's Butter on It

❧

THIS IS REALLY DANIEL'S FAULT. Daniel is four—as smart a four-year-old as *I've* ever played poker with. (He likes to deal twos-and-jacks-and-the-man-with-the-axe.) He's Gill's nephew. We were sitting around Gill's family's Easter dinner, licking our plates clean of turkey, dressing, turnips, mashed potatoes with cream cheese (yum!), when Daniel, out of the blue, said, "Auntie G, how come you're fat?"

She isn't, I should quickly add. She *certainly* isn't now, which I'll get to in a minute, and, to my eye at least, wasn't then. Oh, maybe a little, shall we say, hefty. And there *were* a couple of pairs of the tight jeans she wears on weekends that I hadn't seen for a while. But when a four-year-old, especially one you're crazy about, uses the *real* F-word, there's not much room for discussion. Gill pushed her plate away.

"Daniel!" said Daniel's father, as only fathers can declaim.

"It's all right," said Gill, as frown clouds appeared on Daniel's puzzled brow. Except it wasn't.

"Wednesday," she said on the way home.

"Weight Watchers again, eh?" I said, happy—for the moment—that she'd regained her voice.

"Wednesday," she repeated. "That will give me time to lay in skim milk and fruit and some of those thin wafers. Then I'll get weighed and we'll—"

"*We'll?* He didn't say *I* was—"

"—start Thursday."

"Gee, thanks, Daniel," I said.

THE LAST TIME we'd been through this, I confess, it was as much my decision as hers. I'd just seen one too many pictures of myself in which I looked as if I had a balloon inflated under my sweater. Gill, too—it was her mother who was making remarks that time, though she didn't use the F-word—was unhappy with her appearance. Together, we made some resolutions.

Curiously, our methods turned out to be the inverse of the way we cook. Where I can't even start a dinner without a browse through the cookbooks, and Gill just starts chopping, when we dieted together, she chose a method and I ad-libbed. First, I stopped drinking—even wine. (Gill has the advantage of not drinking anyway.) Then I started leaving the sugar out of the 312 cups of coffee that get me through my radio mornings. As well, and more characteristically, I expanded our shelf of cookbooks— some of which, I suppose, had helped me inflate my balloon in the first place (ever made the Corned Beef with

Cabbage and Horseradish Cream in *Greene on Greens,* with its tablespoon of butter, quarter cup of sour cream and quarter cup of *whipping* cream?)—with a selection of diet books.

In the best of those books, *The Philosopher's Diet: How to Lose Weight and Change the World,* by Richard Watson, I found the key to my own program. "Fat," *The Philosopher's Diet* begins. "I presume you want to get rid of it. Then quit eating so much." I did. I forswore desserts. I skinned my chickens, left the butter off my sandwiches— whole wheat bread, if you please—and the oil out of my salad dressings. I even started eating breakfast: fruit, a boiled egg—*one* boiled egg—and milk with blue veins poured over crunchy cereal, and stopped grazing between meals on anything but celery and apples.

Gill, meantime, signed up at Weight Watchers. All I know about this hugely successful international operation is how well it has worked for her. Twice. Twenty-four dollars to join; twelve dollars a week to be weighed and encouraged. With membership came a number of guides and booklets, the basis of which, it seemed to me, was simply to quantify Richard Watson's succinct "quit eating so much." Weight Watchers divides all foods into six categories: milk, fat, protein, vegetables, bread and fruit, with a catch-all that includes—and gives calorie counts for—such miscellany as capers and corn starch. After her first weigh-in, Gill turned into a kind of recording secretary of the dinner table, noting each item she consumed with the care of an archivist, refusing dressing on her hearts of palm—"I've already *had* my two selections of fat today"—and sauce on her fillet of sole. She, too, started eating breakfast, and going light on lunch.

She also shrank. We both did. Over a couple of months in which we were tiresome dinner guests—"Oh, no, no beans and almonds for us, please, there's *butter* on them!"—we lost a combined total of perhaps thirty pounds. We felt better. I started swimming. Gill got back into her jeans; I bought a new—black—sweater. And then, like almost everyone who's ever completed a diet, we slowly and steadily returned to our more normal, sinful, satisfying ways—though I discovered that I actually *preferred* sugarless coffee.

Until Easter. Easter and Daniel.

WAS I FAT, TOO? Oh, probably. Even without sugar in my coffee, and just one foray into Bert Greene's voluptuous horseradish cream, I certainly hadn't worn that black sweater for a while, and seeing myself on television had made me realize once again how suitably for radio I'm built. Still, over the years, I'd learned to live with myself. I'd relished that spate of newspaper stories about how dieting can be bad for you (well, I'd relished the headlines; I didn't want to know *too* much), and I'd reminded myself that at some periods in our history, a little heaviness around the middle—"a corporation," as my grandfather would have called it—was a sign of distinction.

But when Gill hit the high road again, I was, however unwittingly, dragged to the sidewalk. The trouble with living with a dieter is that you feel guilty all the time. The trouble with shopping with a dieter is that you head inexorably for the Lean Cuisine. And the trouble with cooking with a dieter is that she rules the stove; you can make separate salad dressings, but when I want to microwave the asparagus in chicken stock and Gill wrinkles her nose—"there's fat in it"—guess who wins?

So, as I say, thanks, Daniel. Your Auntie G has lost twenty pounds as I write this. I've lost—well, at least two. We'll see you for dinner at Thanksgiving, if not before, and that fashion model beside you will probably pass on the mashed potatoes. I hope you remember to say something nice to her.

SECRETS OF THE
PREMIER'S SALAD

❧

THE FIRST TIME I encountered the famous Caesar salad that is the pride of the Hon. Joseph A. Ghiz, premier of Prince Edward Island, was on the radio. Mr. Ghiz—it's hard not to call him Joe, as most of the island does—was in the CBC studio in Charlottetown, concocting up a storm. I was in Toronto, surrounded by lettuce, cheese, freshly squeezed lemons, crisp bacon, raw eggs, pepper and the results of my own efforts, the night before, to replicate the premier's garlic-soaked croutons.

It was fun. Joe Ghiz can radiate an infectious enthusiasm, and his delight in his own culinary skills— untramelled in this case, though he didn't fail to tell the world about it, by the lack of a draining board to dry his lettuce in the washroom at CBC Charlottetown—came bubbling down the line. The salad I tossed according to his long-distance instructions? Not bad, if you ask me. *Morningside*'s producers had a pleasantly garlicky lunch that day, and a lot of listeners wrote in for the recipe.

Mr. Ghiz, though—oh, what the heck, Joe—was unsatisfied. "I don't think you *really* got it," he said when we were finished. "The next time you're on the island, I'll *show* you how it's done."

And now, here we were. A whole gang of us. Our annual swing through the Maritimes to play some golf for literacy had begun at the lovely Green Gables course at Cavendish. On the links, we had been joined not only by the premier but by Mrs. Ghiz, the redoubtable Rose Ellen. Rose Ellen is the perfect match for Joe, a winsome, accomplished, occasionally sardonic woman who is as competitive—she won an easy fifty cents from me in our private long-driving contest—as he is devil-may-care. After a pleasant round, enlivened by their mutual teasing and obvious pride in each other, all of us had repaired to the Ghizes' gracious old home on North River Road.

"It's in the kitchen," Joe said conspiratorially as he poured me a glass of wine. "Want to see it?"

JOE GHIZ is a beguiling man. As the son of Lebanese immigrants, he is at once an outsider on his beloved Prince Edward Island—people still remember the racial slurs that accompanied his first election victory—and the quintessential islander: outgoing, straightforward, uncomplicated. Yet the just-another-innocent image he sometimes projects—"What's this al fresco they're serving for lunch?" he had said on the golf course—conceals a canny and well-informed mind. Though he represents, as another premier once told me with a mixture of amusement and admiration, "fewer people than the mayor of

Sarnia, Ontario," he has been an influential player in the constitutional talks of the past several years. And at home, virtually alone among Canadian premiers, he has managed to negotiate an amicable agreement with public-sector workers to accept a cut in wages to help his cash-strapped province weather the tough economy.

This evening, though, politics—and the rest of the world—were incidental to the making of The Salad.

Preparation had begun before we even hit the golf course. First, the croutons, which lay before us now, redolent of garlic. To make them, the premier had cut about half a loaf of good bakery bread into poker-dice-sized cubes. Then he'd melted a generous slab of butter—"the more butter, the better," he maintains—in a heavy pan, and gently crisped his bread cubes to a golden brown. While the croutons sizzled, he'd crushed seven or eight cloves of garlic—his recipe for six people calls for four, and there would be nearly a dozen of us for dinner—into a medium-sized wooden bowl. Then, when the croutons were done, came what he describes as the essential step: he had poured into the bowl a very good olive oil to *exactly* the level of the tops of the bread, and mixed everything together with a wooden spoon.

"You've got to get the garlic spread around," he explained solemnly.

Also earlier, he had washed and meticulously dried—*he* has a draining board—each leaf of four heads of romaine. Now, he tore them into a large bowl, and over the pieces squeezed lemon after lemon.

Again, the solemn explanation: "When you think you

have enough lemon, add that much more again." The same with the pepper and Parmesan, both of which, I can now reveal, the premier buys preground. "It's the quantity that matters," he explained unabashedly. "With the Parmesan, I always say, when you're satisfied you've put too much in—double it."

A cook after my own heart, I contemplated happily. Then crisis struck, and my impression was confirmed.

"Oh, ———," said the premier (even a politician should be allowed to curse in private without a reporter taking notes), "I forgot the bacon. Robert!"

Into the kitchen bounced the Ghizes' strapping son, newly graduated from high school. Together, the three of us layered the bacon with paper towels, and in minutes microwaved it to crisp perfection.

A team effort now. Break four eggs. Splash the yokes over the salad. Hunt for the Worcestershire sauce in the cupboard.

But wait!

There *was* no Worcestershire sauce.

Time for the consultant from the mainland.

"Try some of that hot sauce," I suggested. And in went one, two, three drops, along with the crumbled bacon and the piquant contents of the crouton bowl.

And—at last, and relishing the ceremony—the premier tossed his Caesar salad.

"Well?" he said, offering me the first nibble.

"Wonderful," I proclaimed in all honesty.

A FEW MINUTES LATER, Rose Ellen Ghiz came in from the patio, her part of the evening's cooking (including *her* famous pineapple dessert) having been achieved both earlier and with considerably less to-do. She helped herself to a bowl of The Salad.

I waited, nerves on edge.

"A good one," she announced. "They're not always as good as he maintains, you know. But this is a winner."

I smiled the closest I can muster to a politician's grin. The secret of the late bacon and the missing Worcestershire sauce would be safe, until now, with me.

"We Are Married,
You Know"

ↇ

I OFTEN THINK OF HISTORY in terms of the people I know and, through this long winter and spring of Canadian discontent, when all of us have had to wonder if the alliance between French and English that is at the heart of our country will survive, I have thought a lot about Lise Payette. Lise (it's another mark of the distance between our two solitudes that few of us know her) is a formidable Québécoise. Over the past couple of decades, she has had a great impact on her province's history and culture, and my own occasional encounters with her have seemed to me to sum up how things were going.

I first met her in the early 1970s. She was a broadcaster then, with her own morning show on Radio-Canada. I was the host of *This Country in the Morning,* her opposite number on the English CBC. When *This Country* went to Montreal for a week, my producers arranged for her to sit in with me. She was, I guess, my cohost, except that Lise didn't co- anything, she was Lise: big, blustery, bright as

April sunshine, a bit naughty (at least by my Upper Canadian standards) and unafraid of speaking her mind. She comes from working-class Montreal, the daughter of a bus driver. She had fought her way out of that background, married a journalist, had a couple of kids, got divorced and taken up radio. By the time I met her she was a star.

I liked her a lot. To tell you the truth, though, she kind of discombobulated me. Years later, talking to a magazine writer about the differences between French- and Anglo-Canadian men, she remembered the week she worked with me. "When I came into the studio," she said, "I'd give everybody a kiss. I guess he [I] didn't know what to make of it. He must have been thinking he'd have to tell everything to his wife back in Toronto."

She left radio not long after that to host a late-night television program called *Appelez-moi Lise*. She set her own style there, too, asking the most fearless questions, laughing her gusty laugh when people got embarrassed and, once, adding to an interview with the goalie Ken Dryden by putting on the goal pads and getting the Montreal Canadiens to shoot pucks at her. "I thought she was crazy," Dryden said.

Maybe. But her program was watched by half the people who had their TV sets on, and when the English CBC decided to start up a late-night show, with me as host, one of the models we tried to emulate was *Appelez-moi Lise*. We never did get as good.

She was too smart to stay in television. When the Parti Québécois was searching for high-profile candidates to run in the 1976 election, they signed her up. To her own surprise, she was swept into power on René Lévesque's tide. Lévesque made her a cabinet minister. Once again, she thrived, the female star of a cabinet that, even to those of us who disagreed with its ultimate goal—independent status for Quebec—seemed better educated, more stylish and just smarter than its counterparts in English Canada.

That's when I encountered her the second time. She was a guest on my late-night show, *Ninety Minutes Live*. On camera, I said how sorry I was that she was working so actively for separatism, that I hoped our friendship was a better symbol of how the country could work than the political maelstrom she was caught up in. I can still see her eyes twinkling when she replied: "But first you should figure out who you are, Peter."

Her life went through a lot of twists and turns in the years that followed. In the Quebec referendum campaign of 1980, she made—even for her—an awkward slip of the tongue: trying to make a point about the traditional role of women in Quebec, she insulted the wife of Claude Ryan, the prominent Liberal and federalist. There was a hullabaloo—you may remember the famous "Yvette" rallies—and, though it's probably wrong to say her comments cost her side the vote, they had an effect. After the referendum, she quit politics and took up writing *téléromans,* the phenomenally successful prime-time soap operas of Quebec television. Her series became even more popular than her talk show, and one of her characters—a womanizer named Jean-Paul Belleau—grew so famous that his name became part of the language, a kind of J. R. Ewing of Quebec. In her spare time, she wrote a book of political memoirs, publicly criticized her old leader René Lévesque ("a bum"), narrated a fiercely controversial film about immigration and, with her daughter Sylvie, wrote another *téléroman* even more popular than the first. To search for her equivalent in English-speaking Canada, you'd have to wrap up all of Barbara Frum, Barbara McDougall and Jack Webster—and still you'd come up short.

And then, in the spring of 1990, there she was in a radio studio with me again, in Montreal. We talked a bit about the old days, and, at last, got down to the current state of relations between our halves of the country. Had she followed the fighting over the Meech Lake Accord? Of course. Did she have thoughts about what might happen if it didn't pass? She just looked at me, her eyes—again— twinkling. If it did?

"Then we'd still be married, wouldn't we?" she said.

For a moment, I was stuck for a comment.

"We are married, you know," Lise went on. "We have kids together—the army, the CBC, a lot of kids. Some of them are in trouble—I'm thinking of VIA Rail—but they're still our kids."

In the control room, I could see our technician, a francophone, applauding. When Lise was getting ready to leave, I stood and kissed her. On the cheek. Firmly.

Thinking of the Elder

ONE MONDAY AFTERNOON at Roy Thomson Hall in Toronto: Maestro Andrew Davis, in loosely tailored black pants and stylish grey sports shirt, lifts his baton. A hundred musicians, in sweaters, blouses, jeans and moccasins, peer at their unfamiliar scores. Davis gestures, the timpani thrumps, and at last rehearsal is under way for the world première of *Tales of the Netsilik,* an original work by the Canadian composer Raymond Luedeke, to be played by the Toronto Symphony with narration by—even perched on a stool at Davis's side, as I am now, script in hand, I cannot quite believe this—me.

This all started more than a year ago. The orchestra had recently returned from a tour of the western Arctic. The trip had left as deep an impression on the musicians as their artistry had on the North. To commemorate it, they commissioned a score by Ray Luedeke, whose full-time job is playing clarinet in their woodwind section, but who, at forty-four, is also a rising star of new Canadian music. (He wrote the fanfare that opened Roy Thomson Hall, for instance.) Luedeke, by chance, had been reading some stories collected in the 1920s by the Danish explorer Knud Rasmussen, and when he read them, as he said, he could "hear the music in my head." Someone who knew my own love for the North and who apparently didn't care that I cannot read a note of music and can barely carry a tune suggested I read the text. Foolishly, I think now, gazing out over the 2,800 seats in Roy Thomson Hall, I accepted. I have rented some tails and a white tie from my racetrack friend Nick the Needle, and the orchestra has provided me with a dressing room and parking spot near the artist's entrance. The first performance is Wednesday.

I'm petrified.

Speaking intimately on the radio every morning to three hundred thousand people who can't see me is one thing. Standing in front of a couple of thousand, with no place to hide and one of the world's great symphonies throbbing behind me, is another.

Tuesday afternoon: I cannot believe the progress Davis and the orchestra have made in just twenty-four hours. But, even to my ear, there is a long way to go. Although the players had been given their individual parts long before yesterday's first rehearsal (a copyist took more than six hundred hours to set down all the different scores), putting the whole thirty-five-minute work together for the first time seems an almost impossible job. There is, after all, no record to listen to.

Davis wastes not a moment. He is only a year older

than Luedeke. But, before his recent departure for his native England, he conducted this orchestra for thirteen years. He knows the players the way Glen Sather knows the Edmonton Oilers. They, in turn, both respect and like him. Somehow, he manages to keep the rehearsal going at breakneck speed without ever losing his sense of humour.

"I never thought I'd live to say this," he remarks at one point in what is obviously a musicians' joke, "but I'd like to hear the percussion a little louder."

They are working hard and intensely. But Davis keeps stopping them and starting again. A bar here—"no, no, violas, that's *too* loud"—a passage there. Italian phrases spice his language: *"Divisi"* (which splits sections within the orchestra to handle the trickiest moments); "Take it down from *allegrissimo,*" "Okay, *tutti*" (which means all together). Though the atmosphere is one of polite and friendly professionalism, my head spins. A day away from performance, the music all sounds disjointed to me, and foreign.

What am I doing here?

As the prelude comes to an end, the Maestro nods me my cue. Voice shaking, I begin to read. I have been rehearsing my own part for some weeks now—Ray Luedeke has taken me through while he played piano and we have had private workouts with the percussion section—but I cannot find the right voice. The words are those of a Netsilik elder, who, after some months of getting to know Rasmussen, finally agreed to share some of the people's ancient beliefs and legends with him, and spoke at length one evening in an igloo, while the explorer sat transfixed. I want to speak the elder's words flatly and intimately, the way the northern people I know communicate even the most dramatic of their thoughts. But with the music swelling behind me, I feel obliged to orate. It's all wrong.

Wednesday, one o'clock: On the way to dress rehearsal, Jacques Israelievitch, the orchestra's soft-spoken, French-born concertmaster, pauses by my dressing room.

"Remember," he says. "The people who are coming tonight *want* to like you. This is an evening of pleasure for them, and you're to be part of it."

If anything, he makes me more nervous than ever.

Then, as the orchestra settles in on stage, Ray Luedeke speaks from the podium. He sets the scene in the igloo, as it was more than sixty years ago. As he talks, smiles break out among his colleagues, many of whom, I suspect, have been working extra hard because the piece is by one of them.

Davis gives the downbeat. Miraculously, the orchestra has come together.

"Just before you start," Jacques Israelievitch has told me earlier, "put yourself in the place of that elder. I know it works for me. If I'm going to play Brahms, I think of what it must have been like to be him." Now, as I begin to read, the words seem to speak themselves. I am still no Lorne Green, and any hope that the people who came up with this idea might have had that I would add drama to the text has long dissipated, I'm sure. But it's okay, I think. Not bad.

As the rehearsal ends, the players break into spontane-
ous applause, for Ray, for themselves and, I dare to hope,
for me.

Wednesday evening, on my way to the Hall: Walking down
the corridor of my apartment building, I am as nervous as
I can ever remember being.

"Think of the elder," I tell myself, thinking of the
concertmaster's advice. "It is as if, sixty years later, you
have the honour of bringing the old stories to a southern
audience. The spirit will carry you through."

As I reach the elevator, I am smiling.

I even remember to go back to the apartment and pick
up the pants I will wear with Nick the Needle's tails.

Saturday night, Roy Thomson Hall: We—the orchestra
and I have actually become "we" now—have made it.
Tales of the Netsilik, performed three times, started
strongly and grew better every night. Three curtain calls
Wednesday and Thursday, and tonight, after an evening
off, four. When Ray Luedeke came out tonight, the audience stood, the first time Andrew Davis can remember
that happening to a Canadian composer.

Closing the door on my dressing room, and on my way
to my spot in the artist's lot, I think of the old Inuk who
first told these stories to Knud Rasmussen, and hope he
would be pleased.

JUST VALDY

ɑɔ

IT WAS LATE. Long before Valdy was due on stage, the Yukon sun had set behind the purple mountains. Still August, but under the spacious canopy, where a couple of hundred people had gathered to raise money for White-horse literacy, the air was November cold. And, let's face it, we were tired. We'd been up late the night before in Watson Lake, a small but infectiously enthusiastic community some four hundred and fifty kilometres to the southeast. We'd sung and read for our supper and taken part in an auction. One local entrepreneur had paid $2,100 to have Cynthia Dale caddie for him this morning—my goodness, was it only this morning?—and when that was over, someone else bid $650 for the *Street Legal* jacket she was wearing. In the morning, we'd thrashed and laughed our way around the nine holes carved out of the bush by a former maintenance superintendent on the Alaska Highway.

The evening and the golf in Watson Lake had raised a

fistful of dollars, and now, here in Whitehorse, we were doing it again. After a sumptuous buffet prepared by local volunteers—all the real work for the literacy events we hold across the country is done by volunteers—we sat at picnic tables under the tent. From the stage, we'd been treated to a feast of song and story that ranged from a Yukon band called the Rinkbinders, whose "horn section" is a set of moose antlers, to a hilarious account by Ron MacLean of *Hockey Night in Canada* fame of what it's like to work with Don Cherry. C. David Johnson, Cynthia's off-and-on love interest on *Street Legal,* had read a golfing version of Robert Service's "Spell of the Yukon," which drew a standing ovation. A precocious eleven-year-old had sung a song about trying to figure out why a guy (me) who believes so strongly in literacy spells his name so peculiarly, and other Yukoners had sung or read or recited in English, French and Tutchone or bid, once again, for the services of famous caddies. (Audrey McLaughlin, the leader of the NDP, had gone for slightly less than Cynthia, showing, as she said, "where people have their priorities.") It was, all in all, another wildly successful and profitable evening—but man, was it cold! Midnight now, and you could see each singer's breath. Only about thirty survivors, hugging themselves for warmth, clustered around the picnic tables.

"I think we should wrap this up," I said to no one in particular. "People are exhausted."

"We're not going," said Shelley Ambrose, my faithful assistant, "until Valdy sings."

Valdy. I don't really remember where I first met him.

Probably in the early days of the Winnipeg Folk Festival, where I started going nearly twenty years ago, when my hair was longer and I dressed in jeans. Even then he was a fixture on the music scene, a sometimes bearded (and sometimes not) prototypical folkie: amiable, peace-loving, full of his songs. He was an environmentalist before there was an environmental movement, a back-to-the-lander, a sailor. His trademarks—then and now—were a bandanna around his neck and a pair of bright red trousers. Valdy grew up in Ottawa, where he was Valdemar Horsdal (his father, a prominent portrait photographer, asked him not to use the family name "in show business"), and he lived for a while in Newfoundland, but when I think of him, I think of the West Coast. Now he lives on Saltspring Island and spends his spare time, which is rare, messing about in boats or fixing up his sylvan home.

Over the years, he has sung hundreds of songs thousands of times. He has crossed Canada more often than VIA Rail. People know his "Rock 'n' Roll Song" or his version of Bob Ruzicka's "Dirty Old Man" or some of the pieces he has tossed off on such topical matters as GST and Meech Lake ("Ten Little White Men," he called that), but by the standards of, say, Bryan Adams, he has never really had a hit. He's just Valdy, not so much a star as a classic troubadour—less changed from the time I first met him than anyone else I know. Everything that was good about the sixties and seventies is good about Valdy.

On the plane to Watson Lake, he had been learning a new song. He had a tape in his "Walkperson" and, as the

Chieftain droned over the wilderness with the poplars turning yellow against the jack pine and eagles soaring below us, he'd drummed his fingers and grinned with pleasure. "Stars in your Eyes" it was called and, though its authors—the Americans Tom Paxton and Mark Elliott—had intended it for other purposes, it seemed to Valdy and the rest of us to be a perfect anthem for literacy—about people, as its lyrics said, who "would not take no for an answer."

Now, in the Whitehorse chill, he rose to sing it. "Stars, stars, stars in their eyes, An endless horizon, a miracle prize."

The tent somehow seemed to grow warmer. C. David and Cynthia began to dance on the gravelled floor. Another couple joined them, then another. Suddenly, we were all on our feet, singing and dancing and swaying with the music, and raising our cups in salute.

It didn't feel late any more.

THREE

SUMMER MEMORIES, WINTER DREAMS

∾

THE MOST AMAZING THING that happened to me over the long and gloomy winter only now coming to an end—it is, isn't it?—is that my golf game, which I have been flailing at (with interruptions) for more than forty years, grew suddenly and magically better.

My swing turned smooth. I would start the club back in one easy motion, turning my hips as gracefully as a ballerina's. Then, from the top of my elegant backswing, I would unleash my coiled power, hitting *through* the ball and finishing with my hands high and my belly button aimed squarely at the distant flag. The ball would click off the sweet spot of my driver and split the fairway in a soaring arc, a hundred yards, two hundred, *three* hundred, or float gently through the sunlit air, up and over the highest tree, and downward, downward to the green, biting the tailored grass with laser accuracy, spinning inexorably toward the cup.

And all the long, cold winter, I never missed a putt.

I DID THIS, you understand, without actually playing golf. I improved my game the way gardeners breed their perfect rhododendrons or surfers catch their perfect waves—with winter dreams. I dreamed mine in front of the television set, watching Fred Couples on the dappled southern fairways, or Arnold Palmer, the hope of old guys everywhere, lashing it out over the desert sands, and in my mind playing with them, hitching my pants up Arnie style as, with the fire flickering in the background, I drifted off to sleep.

My best rounds, though, were played in Canada. In my mind, I'd walk a few holes at Royal Colwood on Vancouver Island, where towering Douglas firs turn the fairways into lush cathedrals, hit a couple of tee shots through the thin mountain air of Jasper, Alberta, with the elk grazing in the rough, skip out across the wind-blown prairies—there's an island hole at the Willows, in Saskatoon, where I actually *did* drift a five-iron onto the water-surrounded green one summer—and head east, pausing only at the Chaudière, in Aylmer, Quebec, to try fecklessly to hit one across the Ottawa River, before I took off for the Atlantic provinces: Green Gables on Prince Edward Island, with each lovely hole named after a Lucy Maud Montgomery character or location, Brightwood, in Dartmouth, Nova Scotia, with its spectacular harbour view, Mactaquac in New Brunswick, its layout as rolling as its name, and, to complete my round, Twin Rivers, in Newfoundland, where salmon fishermen in the rushing streams that line the fairways wear hard hats to ward off wayward balls.

IN TRUTH, of course, the only amazing thing about my golf game is how consistently lousily I've played all these years. I started out all right—or so it seems now. I caddied for my grandfather, and, when I could, started hitting a few myself. Soon, I was taking it seriously. I played to win. Practised, studied—even played a few tournaments, though the only trophies that have survived seem to feature the phrase "runner up." Kept at it, too, till marriage intervened. Went out one day to see if I could still handle it, sliced my first three drives out of bounds, got mad, and, when I finished the round feeling more tense than when I had begun, wondered what I'd ever seen in it, and quit.

Now, or so I tell myself, I play for different reasons. I picked up golf again when I came back to the corner of the world where I had spent the happiest years of my childhood, and found enjoyment in it I had not known before. Now, I confess I'd *like* to be better—and anyone who knows me knows my winter dreams express a real desire—but, well, I know I probably never will be, and, I try to ask myself, who cares? Instead of trophies, I play (I say) for the sun on the back of my neck, the spring of the turf, the bird songs in the air, and, most of all, the sense of the land.

My favourite venues—and I play these all winter, too—are not the famous landmarks, or necessarily even the best "tests of golf." I like courses that are *of* the land they're made from: Chester, in Nova Scotia, where wild roses bloom along the seashore and you gaze out across the islands of Mahone Bay. Or Pender Harbour, on the Sunshine Coast of British Columbia, where you need either to rent a cart to get up the hills or have a mountain goat for a caddie. Or, more than the lavish Willows of Saskatoon, any of a dozen prairie courses where the real hazards are the steady three-fairway wind and the souvenirs of geese that speckle the greens. Or—and maybe most of all—Greenway's Greens, at Watson Lake in Yukon, nine holes bulldozed from the virgin bush by a retired highway superintendent named Bob Greenway, who grew tired, as he said, of taking three weeks a year in North Carolina and leaving his clubs in his closet the rest of the year. I've played all these courses in the last few years, and many more. And every one of them has brought me to my knees.

When summer comes—and it will, it will—I'll play them all again, and, as I do every year, find new ones to test my faltering skills. I'll walk the land and feel the wind. I'll hack and flub and slice and scramble, and grin with pleasure as I go.

But all winter long, it's been a different game, and only Fred and Arnie know how well, at last, I've played.

THE INCREDIBLE
SHRINKING MAN

∾

IF FRIENDS ARE just the people you exchange Christmas gifts with, or have over for supper, or borrow five bucks from when you can't get to the bank machine, then Dennis Kaye, who lives in Quathiaski Cove, British Columbia, is not really a friend of mine. But if, as well, friends are people you just like or admire or wish you knew better, then Dennis Kaye, in spite of the fact that I have never met him—or, for that matter, talked to him on the phone—is. My friend, certainly, and maybe my hero, too.

Dennis is thirty-seven. He is—or was—five feet ten, with brown hair and blue eyes (I know this from his letters) and a body that was once healthy enough to support him and his family by running "the barge," a sixty-foot aluminum hull on which he used to move heavy goods among the lovely and isolated islands around Kelsey Bay.

When he was twenty-nine, Dennis was diagnosed as

having ALS: amyotrophic lateral sclerosis, or, as a lot of people still call it, Lou Gehrig's disease. The reason I'm not sure about his current height is that his body is wasted now, and when he writes to me, as he does every couple of months, laboriously typing out each word with a wand attached to his forehead, he signs himself "The Incredible Shrinking Man." When he gets out of bed these days—or, more properly, when his wife, Ruth, gets him out of bed—he lives in a motorized wheelchair, which, as he says, "goes like hell." I remember the letter about the chair's arrival in his life. "It was great!" he wrote. "The kids tied their tricycle to the back, so with one daughter clinging to my seat, the other riding chariot-style on the trike and me playing Mario Andretti, we were off on the famous 'Q Cove Grand Prix.'

"It's hard to explain," he added wistfully, "how wonderful it felt to be the source of my children's amusement again."

ALS, which strikes about seven out of every hundred thousand of us, kills as many people as muscular dystrophy, multiple sclerosis, cystic fibrosis and Huntington's disease combined. Yet we know very little about it. We don't know what causes it and we certainly don't know how to cure it. As Dennis explains, it's a disease that attacks the motor centre at the base of the brain and, in turn, slowly robs you of voluntary muscle control. "The doctors say," he wrote once, "that the end will come when the muscles controlling my lungs are affected. With a keen mind, a healthy heart and open eyes, I will suffocate."

How long will that be? No one knows. When Dennis was first diagnosed—thirty is unusually young—he was told he had three to five years ("you probably won't out-live your dog"). But Stephen Hawking, the brilliant British scientist, has been living with one form of ALS (not Dennis's) for more than twenty years, and Dennis is—well, Dennis. As Ruth says, he's stubborn.

But there's more than that, I think. Dennis is a very funny man. He finds humour even in what has happened to him. And that, I'm sure, is what keeps him going. "How long does it take a person with ALS to put in a light bulb?" he wrote to me once. "Answer: I'll keep you posted." Or (this from just before he got his wheelchair, when he used to compare trying to walk with having to be on stilts all the time): "One evening I was headed for the bathroom and ended up in the bedroom. I was wob-bling along, minding my own business, and suddenly, for reasons I can't explain, my stilts parted in the middle. The rest was history! I remember saying goodbye to myself in the mirror as I left the bathroom on an unscheduled flight. Thank God for walls. A couple of swanlike twirls later, I ended up spread-eagled on top of our bedside table. As I lay there like some turtle with his shell on back-wards, I heard this sarcastic voice inside me say, 'And now, for my next trick.'"

Last summer, Dennis and what he calls his "small but unstoppable circle of friends" decided to hold an art auc-tion in Victoria to raise money to fight ALS. No one thought they could bring it off. And when they sold some seventy pieces of donated art for more than $20,000,

Dennis wrote, with typical spirit, "It would be juvenile of me to gloat, so, instead, to all the naysayers, I offer these timeless words of profundity and wisdom—five words to be exact—Na na, na na na!" Then, to give Ruth a break—from the hundreds of things she now has to do for him that make the disease an affliction to her life, as well—he checked in to a hospital for a while.

So no, I haven't met him. And no, we won't exchange Christmas presents. But every funny, rich, brave and outrageous letter he writes to me is a gift of sorts. And, if this little salute to him makes anyone think of doing something so that other people in the future can escape what he's going through, then maybe I've returned a bit of the friendship I feel.

Merry Christmas, Dennis Kaye.

THE GREAT GREAT GREAT GREAT GRANDCHILDREN OF SIR CASIMIR, I

∾

My second grandchild is scheduled to arrive in the world on December twentieth, so that although he—or she, of course, though we already have a she—may not be *quite* ready for the turkey dinner, my Christmas will be rich. I *like* being a grandfather, as regular readers of this column know, and never more so than at Christmas. With my own kids grown to sophistication—and to sleeping in—I need someone around me who believes in Santa Claus, and who thinks that anyone still in bed at Christmas dawn has wasted half the day.

The only thing better than having a grandchild, in my prejudiced view, is being one. Especially at Christmas. Christmas is the only time you need your granny as much as when you're sick, when you lie in bed hoping for a mustard plaster.

Grandparents give you a sense of time and where you come from. On my office wall hangs a picture of the perfect Stephanie, the granddaughter I write about all the time, wearing a sailor suit and a wide-brimmed hat, which she is holding, fetchingly, as if against the wind. Above that is one of me that, because I'm flapping my arms like an osprey and have a cigarette dangling from my fingers, the CBC doesn't want to publish. Above that, in turn, is *my* grandfather, Lieutenant-Colonel H. N. Gzowski, an engineer who ran a gas station for the last twenty years of his life, and whom I loved inordinately. And above the Colonel is *his* grandfather, Sir Casimir Stanislaus Gzowski, the Polish aristocrat who came to this country in 1842 as a refugee and started the whole line—a six-generation span on a couple of feet of wallboard. Like Stephanie, Sir Casimir, who has mutton chop whiskers, is wearing a military outfit—a soldier suit, in his case—and he, too, is holding his hat, which appears to have a bad-minton bird on the top.

The Colonel, Stephanie's great-great-grandfather, died long before she was born. But I will tell her—and her new brother or sister when the time is right—stories: how he taught me how to swear (*no one* could swear like the Colonel) and to print, in my childish hand, the letters engineers use in draughting, strong on the vertical, soft on the cross strokes. When I do that, I'll be echoing the tales the Colonel told me years ago, of the old soldier with the mutton chops, Stephanie's great-great-great-great-grandfather, whom *he* remembered as a gruff, tall man with a funny accent, who used to bounce him on his knee.

Grandparent to grandchild, grandparent to grandchild.

It's as if we skip the generations between, and pass the stories of our families down the line.

My view of grandparents is, as I say, prejudiced. I had more than my share. It was one of the good things (there were a few) about being a child of divorce-and-remarriage. My arrangement came with three complete sets: my mother's parents, my birth father's (no couple of that time would lose touch with a grandchild over such a little matter as the breakup of their son's marriage) and my stepfather's parents, for whom I, their first grandson, may have helped to mitigate the disappointment of their son's having married a divorcée.

Divorces in Canada were as rare as cocktail lounges in the early forties, so my situation, common now, was a rare one. I garnered more birthday presents than any kid I knew, more personal letters that smelled of lavender (my mother had me take her second husband's name, Brown, but my grandmother would pointedly address her envelopes to Peter John *Gzowski* Brown) and, best of all, more Christmas dinners. More than once, I remember, I began the holiday with dinner at noon with my step-family in Galt, was driven the sixty miles to Toronto, where I would be dropped off at the Gzowskis' (many of whose men, including my father, were away at war), and then, finally, be picked up again to join my mother's family, the Youngs, for a third helping of plum pudding.

It's hard to imagine women more different from each other than my grandmothers. But each, in her own way, was as perfect as Stephanie is now.

Grandmother Brown was quiet and gentle and warm, a cookie magician with soft flannel sheets on the beds where I sometimes slept over.

Grandmother Gzowski—"Danny" to me and my cousins and eventually to everyone in her family—was the Colonel's lady, who before her marriage had travelled in Europe and North Africa with her older sister, a noted concert singer (till her dying day she gave endearingly perfect French pronunciations to such words as "restaurant" and "carton"), and, later kept house for the Colonel everywhere from a gravel pit on Vancouver Island to a third-floor walk-up in Toronto—always immaculately and with grace. She could play tennis like Mo Connolly, bridge like Helen Sobel (the Colonel, by contrast, used what we dubbed the "Massey-Harris system"—anything his partner bid he raised to three no trump), was a gifted photographer and made the best roast lamb in the world.

And then there was Grandma Young, first woman graduate of the University of Manitoba, first woman to have an Ontario driver's licence (which she exercised to others' peril well into her eighties), headstrong, opinionated, and as independent as Auntie Mame. Grandma Young lived alone into her nineties, and was not well off—she had lost most of her lawyer-husband's earnings on the stock market in 1929—but Christmas dinner at *her* house was served on Royal Doulton china, with antique silver settings. Even when there was no money to pay the gas bill, she wore a velvet dress at Christmas, and served pale sherry from a crystal carafe.

In her day, Grandma Young had known four governors-general by their first names, and once, in Washington, she told me, President Warren Gamaliel Harding pinched her on the . . .

But enough. These are family stories, *grandparents'* stories, and I should save them till some future Christmas, to tell Stephanie and the one who's due this year.

Do you think he—or she—would like a hockey stick for Christmas, by the way? Or is it just a touch too soon?

THE GREAT GREAT ETC., II

❧

"He," in case you've been holding your breath for a year, turned out to be she after all—Miss (still too young for a Ms, don't you think?) Samantha Hailey Gzowski Zufelt, a perfect little brunette sister for the equally perfect blonde Stephanie Anne, and therefore, of course, a second perfect grandchild for me.

Samantha was born on Christmas Eve, 1990, just after I wondered if her first Christmas—or his, as might still have been the case—was too soon for a hockey stick. She's still too young for hockey, I suppose. She may not even have quite figured out what Christmas is yet—you know how babies get swamped with presents while we all stand around hoping they'll stop for a minute and play with *ours*. ("But she *loved* your teddy bear, Uncle Jack.") But she'll smile a lot anyway. Smiling is a habit of Samantha's—when, that is, she's not working on a new tooth or wanting to have her laundry changed. She's good at it. She's good at a lot of things. Why, when she was six months old she—

Boring, aren't we, we grandparents? We think we're the first people ever to *have* grandchildren—and so young, too, you're supposed to point out, as in, "My, you don't *look* like a grandfather."

Forgive us. Looking at those snapshots—"yes, that could be your nose, the poor dear, but she has her father's colouring, don't you think?"—won't hurt you, you know. Just . . . well, smile, and use the word "adorable" if you can. And even if you've heard the story before— about, for instance, the Christmas Stephanie was Samantha's age, still working on her first words, and sitting next to me at the dinner table, reached out to tug my beard, grinned happily and said, clear as a bell, "Doggie"—even if you've heard it before, be patient; at least stories about kids' sayings are short.

Anyway, we don't talk about them as much as you think. It just seems that way. It's a full year, in fact—twelve whole columns—since I've even mentioned my grandchildren in these pages. But here it is Christmas again, and inevitably a person's thoughts—not only a grandparent's—turn to families, and to kids.

I CAN'T BELIEVE how much families have changed in my lifetime. When I was a kid, as a child of divorced parents, I was an oddity. The year I was twelve, five thousand Canadian marriages were dissolved (most of them by the Senate; remember that?), but none of them, so far as I could tell (except, of course, for my own parents'), was in Galt. None of my friends could figure out how I came to have three sets of grandparents—my mother's parents, my stepfather's and my birth father's—or how, though I went by my stepfather's name (anything else would have been just too confusing in Galt), I was still, legally, someone else. "Family" to my friends, and especially at Christmas, meant grandma and grandpa at the ends of the table, and father, mother, uncles, aunts and cousins stretched out down the sides, everyone with the same last name.

Today, I'd be almost the norm. Not only divorce, but separation, remarriage, common-law arrangements, single parenthood and various other permutations have reshaped our lives. Fewer than a third of Canadian families now fit the old pattern of two parents (first marriage) with one wage earner. One in four children lives in a home without a father. (I know three different women who have raised kids, by choice, on their own.) The jolly old scene of grandparents and uncles has given way to one of step-siblings and new partners, shifting relationships or, sometimes, of just Mom and the kids alone. It's often just as jolly, mind you, but it's *different*.

I'm a case in point. This Christmas Eve, I'll go to my cousin's house, where a lot of people, some related, some not, drop in for eggnog and carols. Gill will be there, and so will my kids and their various partners and, we all hope, their mother—although, to be frank, we haven't yet reached the stage of civilization where the ex- and the current spouse are *friends*. On the day itself, Gill will go to her parents' place to join her relatives (Gill's family is still pretty close to the traditional picture), and I'll be at the house where my ex-wife lives, with our kids, their kids—that's just Stephanie and Samantha for now—and, again, their various companions. After we open presents, some of us will take off for other combinations and other dinners. It's a whirlwind and, in all honesty, there are sometimes strains.

But know something? It's always worth it—worth every minute. One of the other realities of modern life is that even the families whose patterns haven't changed don't hang out together as much as they used to. I can't prove this statistically, of course, and it may well be that, living in a big city, divorced and resettled, with a job whose schedule keeps my extracurricular life to a minimum (unless, that is, you want to have breakfast with me at five o'clock in the morning), I am, once again, outside the common pattern. But it still seems to me that such institutions as family outings, family games, family conferences—family *gatherings*—are losing their place in our lives, giving way to travel, parties, clubs, movies and just plain busyness.

Except, thank heavens, for Christmas. In whatever new configurations, we do get together then—as families. We spend time with each other, catch up with what's happened, tell old stories, play old games. And at the centre are the children.

At Christmas, the children are more than just themselves. They're memories, too—of holidays past, of other children before them, and most of all of our own lost childhood. They take us back to the families we grew up in, and the warmth that spreads from our love for them makes all the changes in our lives seem unimportant.

So Merry Christmas, Samantha Hailey Gzowski Zufelt. You'll get that hockey stick one of these years, if you want it, and a lot of other presents, too. But I wonder if you'll ever know how much you give us in return.

GAMES OF OUR LIVES

~

W<small>HEN I WAS A YOUNG FATHER</small>—a yuppie, I guess, except we didn't have those in the sixties—one of my annual Christmas shopping stops was at a store in Toronto called Mr. Gameways. Every year, I would buy at least one commercial game there, picking up the latest fad—or attempt to start a fad—in a box.

We would open the box on Christmas Eve. After our ritual take-out Chinese dinner, and after the kids had each opened the one present we allowed them before Santa arrived, we'd puzzle out the rules of our new game and play a round or two to divert them until it was time to try to get them to bed. On Christmas Day, if the game was a good one, we'd break it out again and use it to fill the long hours between the opening of the real presents, with all those trips upstairs to try on the new sweater or perform a first experiment on the new chemistry set, and the presentation of the turkey and the plum pudding.

A few of the games survived beyond their Christmas

unveilings. Risk, I remember, a Parker Brothers card-and-dice war that involved deploying your armies around a map of the world—"I'm attacking Yakutsk"—spread from our family into the circle of my oldest son's friends and lasted well into the rainy summer. Tuf, with dice whose faces displayed numbers and mathematical symbols, which you tried to shape into increasingly complex equations, lasted (surprisingly) for at least three Christmases. And Clue, probably the most successful commercial invention of the time—"Is it Colonel Mustard in the library with a candlestick?"—earned a place on our games shelf alongside such classics as Monopoly, Scrabble or—now—Trivial Pursuit, which is, surely, in a league by itself.

The majority, though, barely made it to Christmas afternoon. Snap Judgment, Payday, Stratego, Probe, Astro Blitz, Krypto, Pit—even their names have sunk into disuse. Their rules, if we ever did figure them out, are now long forgotten.

THAT WAS, AS I SAY, a long time ago. I'm an old father now (and a grandfather, though the perfect Stephanie Anne Gzowski Zufelt is still too young for games), and I would no more *buy* a game to play with my now-grown family these days—always excepting, of course, a new edition of Trivial Pursuit—than I would pay money to go for a walk in the winter air with them. I have, in my maturity, realized what I might well have known all along, that the best games in life are free—except perhaps for the price of some things you already have around the house.

The best of them all, I think (though I have a few more up my sleeve) is the one called, in my family as in many others, Dictionary. There are, I've noted recently (though Mr. Gameways has long since closed its doors), some commercial versions of Dictionary around, with fancier names and pre-packaged clues. Forget 'em. All you need to play this sprightliest of family word games is a standard dictionary (though the bigger it is the better your game will be), paper, pencils and some imagination.

Any number can play, though three is probably too few and you won't want more than eight or nine. For each turn, one player is "It." "It" begins by picking an obscure word from the dictionary—so obscure that no one in the game could know its real meaning. (If anyone does, in fact, he should say so, and "It" should try again.) "It" reads the word aloud. Each player tries to make up a definition that sounds plausible. (A tip here is to keep your attempt as simple as possible, though some of the best players I know will slip in a bit of mock dictionary-ese.) All the players pass their definitions to "It," who then reads them aloud in random order—and mixes in, somewhere, the real one. Then everyone except "It" votes. You get ten points if you pick the real definition, and five each time someone votes for yours. (Some people play a variation that allows you to vote for your own definition and earn a safe one point.) If everyone misses, "It" gets twenty.

And that's all. You add up the points, and "It" passes the dictionary to the next player for a new round.

Here, as an example, is a round from a game I played a

while ago. The word was "teel," which means—well, try it. One (but only one) of these definitions is real.

1) **teel** (*naut.*): the longest reach of a tack before the wind;

2) **teel** (*Scot.*): a mixture of oats and barley used to make the mash for whiskey;

3) **teel** (*Hindi*): the oil of sesame seed;

4) **teel**: the cap that covers the screws on a propeller;

5) **teel** (v.): to tickle;

6) **teel**: the nap of Irish linen.

The right answer? I'm tempted to send you to the dictionary—you'd be amazed at how many playable words there are and how easily they lend themselves to fanciful definitions—but since I'm in a holiday mood, teel is really, Hindi origin and all, the oil of sesame seed. If you guessed that, remember, you'd have earned ten points, and if you'd made up one of the others, or one even more able to entice your opponents, you'd earn five for each person who guessed wrongly.

Simple, eh? And, I remind you, free. Even though the kids no longer have to be distracted from pre-Christmas tension, our family has been playing it in the blank spaces of holidays for years, and we enjoy it more, I think, every time.

But if we grow weary of it this year, or if, as sometimes happens, the only dictionary we can find is too small to contain the right kind of tantalizing word—I still remember "demurrage," which came up in the same game as "teel," and which someone fooled me on by offering the hauntingly lovely definition of "an inexplicable sorrow" ("demurrage" is in fact what a freight carrier is entitled to if his delivery is delayed)—we can always try a new game some friends of mine, stuck at a cottage without a dictionary, invented this summer. It's called Encyclopedia. You look up someone in the *Canadian Encyclopedia*—Frederick Montizambert, say, who's on page 1156 of the blue edition—and people try to guess what he's in there for.

It beats Stratego every time.

Four Hours and One Knockdown Later

THIS IS ABOUT BREAD, but, with apologies to earlier writers who combined loaves and fishes, I can't make my point unless I tell you first about my friend Jake, who every spring goes after the great salmon of New Brunswick or Labrador. Gets 'em, too. Flies to a private camp—Jake is a very successful lawyer—ties a few flies, misses a few shaves, clambers into hip waders, forgets the problems of corporate litigation and emerges a few days later with enough pink Atlantic flesh to spread among those of us who have had to stay at home.

Once I invited him for a feast of his own bounty, which I'd barbecued in tin foil, stuffed with lemon, tomatoes and oodles of fresh dill. Delicious, we all agreed, and free, too.

"Free?" said Jake. "If you count airfare, whisky and maybe a quarter of the court time I lost, those fish run about $300 a pound."

ANYWAY, BREAD.

I decided to make some this past winter. Over Christmas, I'd acquired some new food books, and nearly every one had at least a chapter on the pleasures and satisfactions of baking. With all the dismal news of the winter, I thought I could use the therapy of kneading. And, with the economy in recession, making my own food seemed a prudent thing to do.

I may, in fact, have hit on a new social trend. Certainly the man in the bulk-food store where I went to stock up on stone-ground flour and unpackaged yeast thought so. "I hate to say it," he said, "but bad times make good business for us."

With my flour and yeast, I headed to the hardware store for measuring spoons, spatulas, baking sheets for baguettes, pans for higher loaves. From the supermarket, more yeast (fast-rising, just in case), milk, sugar, corn meal for the baking sheet.

Next morning, I spread out three of the books that had tempted me: James Beard's *Delights and Prejudices,* Laurie Colwin's *Home Cooking* and a memoir called *Potboiler* by Robert Canzoneri, who, being grey-bearded and a self-described amateur, strikes a chord with me. While each had its flaws , I managed to make a kind of all-star recipe from all three, half whole-wheat flour, half all-purpose. After proofing my bulk yeast in warm water, I realized that (a) most recipes call for "a package" of yeast; (b) Fleischmann's, bless their hearts, put the quantity on their packages only in grams, while (c) my measuring spoons were in teaspoons, so that (d) I didn't know how to measure the bulk yeast and settled for an envelope of Fleischmann's fast-rising.

I made my dough, using, I figured later, too much of my half-water, half-milk, and looking, as a result, as if I were taking a course in papier-mâché sculpture. Added more flour, scraped off the counter, dusted my hands and began the highly satisfying process of kneading. Wonderful! Punched down my dough a final time, stuck it in a bowl with a clean towel over the top and settled in to the cryptic crossword.

Four hours and one knockdown later (I knocked the dough down, not my hopes) I had a baguette you could drive nails with and a bigger loaf that was—well, it wasn't bad toasted.

Back to basics. The next weekend it was time for Fannie Farmer, in the new version of her *Baking Book* brought up to date "for our generation" by Marion Cunningham. Foolproof. I followed Fannie-Marion's directions to the letter, from warming my mixing bowl to measuring out the flour—all white, this time—precisely half a cup at a time. I kneaded for eight minutes by the clock and let the dough rise a full two hours before the knockdown, another one and a half after it. I did everything *exactly* right, in other words, and I got two loaves of—well, it was better than my all-star recipe, but, except for the warmth, it wasn't much—if any—better than what I can get at the local bakery for $1.89 a loaf. To tell you the truth, it didn't even *smell* like fresh-baked bread.

It was time for the ultimate weapon—ultimate in my

arsenal, anyway. I called Elizabeth Baird. Elizabeth, helpful as always—I sometimes wonder if even the readers of
Canadian Living know what a font of knowledge she
is—had just the solution: the perfect bread recipe she had
found in a course some years ago.

Here are the secrets I know now (thanks to Elizabeth):
Just the *tiniest* bit of sugar (a teaspoon) so that the yeast is
allowed to act on the flour. Add ¼ cup of skim milk powder to the dough, and beat it all—2½ cups of lukewarm
water, 5½ cups of all-purpose flour, the sugar, milk powder, a tablespoon of salt—with an *electric* mixer, starting
with 3 cups of the dry mixture and adding the remainder
gradually. Knead for at least ten minutes. "Give yourself a
workout," as Elizabeth says. Let it rise the first time as long
as two and a half hours—till it's *tripled* in bulk—and
knock it down not once but twice, letting it double each
of the last two times. Cut some slashes into the tops of
your baguettes and, to get a real French crust, heat your
oven to 425°F (220°C), and just before you enter your
loaves—you should have four—slip in a baking pan with
an inch of cold water in the bottom. Bake for twenty to
twenty-five minutes, till the loaves sound hollow.

This works. The kitchen actually smelled like fresh
bread. We ate one loaf as soon as it was cool enough to
hold, and with another sopped up the dregs of my, ahem,
world-famous stew.

That evening, I added up the cost of the measuring
spoons, baking pans, unused milk powder, corn meal,
flour, electric mixer, the gas for all those shopping trips

and, using Jake's formula, about a quarter of what I might have earned at the typewriter or on the radio while I was baking or waiting for the dough to rise.

It came to—well, it *was* cheaper than the salmon.

Leon to the Rescue

◡

"You have to go to wardrobe," Shelley said.

"Wardrobe?"

"For a suit."

"But I'm playing me, aren't I?" I said. "I don't wear suits."

"Well," Shelley said, "it's *sort* of you, but—"

Shelley—Shelley Ambrose—is, formally, my assistant. More accurately, she is my manager, travel agent and correspondence secretary. In short, she runs my life, and, usually, she's my friend. This time, however, I wasn't so sure.

A month or so earlier, we'd had a call from the producers of *Street Legal*. A couple of seasons ago, they'd shot a scene in which Eric Peterson, as Leon Robinovitch, had appeared on *Morningside,* and except for having to have my hair blow-dried into a kind of hair-spray helmet, I'd had quite a good time. Now, they told Shelley, they wanted me again.

Sure, we'd told them after a quick huddle. Anything to, ahem, help their ratings. They sent a script over. I put it in a drawer—we quick studies don't need to peek ahead. Now, however, it was the day before shooting. And— well, when I actually looked at the script, my character turned out to be a *bit* like me (he was to moderate a panel at a public meeting in his brief appearance) but his name was Peter Sibella, not Gzowski. Furthermore, in an earlier version—the pros at *Street Legal* send you all the drafts—he'd been *Hannah* Sibella, convincing me that I was, at best, second choice for the role, behind Hannah Gartner of *the fifth estate.*

Whatever the case, Peter wore suits.

"Wardrobe," Shelley repeated. "Be there at two."

"I guess it's too late to get out of it," I said.

NEXT DAY, terrified and self-conscious, but at least properly outfitted—and looking kind of spiffy, if I say so myself, with my borrowed tie Scotch-taped to my borrowed shirt, and my hair, once again, blown to dry perfection—I stood on the platform at St. Lawrence Hall, in downtown Toronto. Grips and technicians busied themselves all round me with lights and cameras. The room swirled with extras, swarming back and forth across the aisles, responding to the shouted instructions of directors and ADs—assistant directors, of which *Street Legal* has five—to give the illusion of a crowded auditorium. On the platform with me were a couple more of the extras, in non-speaking roles just to fill the chairs and—oh, dear, as if I weren't intimidated enough—Gordon Pinsent, one of the giants of Canadian drama, who like many other Canadian stars before him, was making a guest appearance on *Street Legal,* in his case as a villainous immigration official, who would, when the scene unfolded, be questioned from the audience by the earnest and dedicated Leon Robinovitch.

This was the walk-through, as the director planned her shots. In its fifth season, *Street Legal* has become a well-oiled machine. At other locations earlier in the day, the crews had shot scenes called "Alana Trusts Barbara," and "Alana Disrobes," which, for all the program's occasional sexiness, turned out to be nothing more than a few lines of dialogue recorded while the character played by Julie Khaner gets out of her judge's garb.

At St. Lawrence Hall, for "Leon Embarrasses [the Pinsent character]," not a moment was wasted. The whole scene would last perhaps a minute and a half in the finished product, but each line had to be shot three or four times—up close, over someone's shoulder, from behind the platform—so that, later, the editors could keep the action moving. For each shot, lights had to be moved, extras redistributed. There was room for tension, but little for mistakes. Under my fancy getup, butterflies flew.

But not for long.

In the scene, Peter Sibella (me) was to ask the man firing the penetrating questions from the audience whether he has "more than a casual interest" in the matter under dispute. The man, of course, is the character played by

Eric Peterson, who had learned that morning he had once again been nominated for an award for his work on stage—the steady income from a popular series subsidizes a lot of more serious acting in this country—and in reading it, Peterson managed, without breaking the rhythm of the rehearsal, to make such a production out of "My name is Leon Robinovitch and I am a lawyer" (he sounded like Mighty Mouse, arriving to save the planet), that all over the set smiles broke out, and even the extras relaxed.

Then, as we waited on the platform, Gordon Pinsent began whispering such good-natured asides to me ("If you speak slowly, the camera has to stay on you longer—that's why John Wayne talked like that") that even *I* began to feel at home.

And, best of all, Peterson, aware of my discomfort at being called upon to *act,* "accidentally" called my character "Mr. Gzowski." Watching, one of the writers shrugged. "Leave it," she said.

Right on schedule, the cameras rolled. Peterson and Pinsent, who had passed the time between set-ups bouncing their lines off each other—so convincingly that once when I approached them I thought they were in serious private conversation—and running through some old Noel Coward duets (each is also an accomplished singer), carried the rest of us along on their professionalism. Having to "act" between them was like having to help the Harlem Globetrotters play basketball. However woodenly, I spoke all five of my lines without a stumble.

Still on schedule, the director called a wrap, as we say in show business.

I took my suit back to wardrobe.

"How did it go?" asked Shelley the next day.

"Not badly," I said. "Did Hollywood call?"

ROYAL FLUSH

෬

INEVITABLY, I SUPPOSE—or suppose now when I
have the advantage of hindsight and have become, ahem,
a veteran of royal engagements—when I actually got to
speak to him, I said something inane.

He, of course, is The Prince. Not *a* prince, the sort
they had in Calgary the same weekend, but *The Prince*—
Charles himself, heir to the throne, the future king,
Charles the—what?—III, if the monarchy lasts. Meanwhile, The Prince. In Toronto.

"How do you do," I think he said.

"Your Royal Highness," I said, as I'd been prepared to
say, dipping my head in the token bow I'd decided would
be—no, dammit, now that I think of it, I forgot to do
that. I just shook his hand, gently.

"And will you be there tomorrow?" The Prince said,
opening the door for my blunder.

I would, in fact, be seeing him the next day. He and
The Princess were the stars of a huge gala in Toronto.

Because some of the money their presence would raise would go to literacy, I had been signed on as master of ceremonies, and to tell you the truth, I was pretty excited about it. But instead of a simple "Yes, sir, looking forward to it," I plunged into a long, scarcely coherent ramble about how I'd use the opportunity of being on my feet to make a long speech about the Canadian identity—oh, forget it. I was trying to be funny. It didn't come off.

Didn't bother The Prince, though. He smiled anyway, as if I'd actually been amusing, and moved on down the line, shaking hand after hand and listening, I imagine, to still more inanities. My guess, after a couple of days of royal watching, is that nearly every one of the thousands of people The Prince and his family meet as they travel around the world spend the first few minutes after their royal encounter saying to themselves, "Oh, no, did I *really* say that?"

If my experience is typical, it's no wonder. In the late twentieth century, the British royals are the pre-eminent celebrities in the world, bigger than television, larger than life. Otherwise sensible people go gaga over their activities and weak-kneed in their presence. I have a friend, an important executive in the oil patch, who subscribes to *Monarchy* magazine—it's *all* about the royals—and stays up late to watch their every appearance on television. My oldest daughter, world traveller, about-to-be-published author, arose early the morning Charles and Diana were getting married and put on white gloves to watch the ceremony by satellite. When that same couple, parents now, were in Toronto last fall, Shelley Ambrose, who is normally level-headed, skipped a morning's work to jump up and down at City Hall. "I was *ten feet* from her," she said breathlessly when she got back. "She's *gorgeous!*"

Half the people I talked to were at least as worked up as Shelley. When I went shopping to prepare for the royal weekend—sputtering at every stop, I confess, that I was among those who would get to shake the royal hand—(1) the shoe repairman wouldn't accept a fee for putting a gloss on my scruffy black pumps, (2) Carmen, the world's best barber, pumped so much hair spray into my coiffure that I felt as if I were wearing a helmet, and (3) the clerk in the haberdashery where I went—do you *believe* this?—to buy a new formal shirt for the gala had a hard time concentrating on finding my size—the royal cavalcade had just driven past his store and he was sure The Prince had waved at him.

The only people I ran into all weekend who weren't in a flap, in fact, were the royals themselves—though I can, I should say, vouch only for Charles, since my experience of Diana consisted of watching her walk across the dance floor toward her table at the Saturday night gala, wearing a stunning green and black evening gown while flash-bulbs popped like noisy fireflies and I read nervously into the microphone.

The place where I was introduced, and made my silly speech, was at the headquarters of a literacy group called YES CANADA, a remarkable organization that works with school dropouts. After going through the receiving line and having a bit of a walkabout, The Prince settled in with a group of YES CANADA "associates" (they avoid the word students) for a session I'd been asked to moderate. The associates, mostly in their late teens, and with a variety of colourful backgrounds, were a-tingle with excitement—as much a result of how the program's organizers had briefed them, I imagine, as of their own sense of awe, and each, somewhat to my dismay—I was hoping for some spontaneity—had come armed with a couple of carefully thought-out written questions to pop His Royal Highness.

No problem. After some perfunctory introductions, The Prince simply—and guilelessly—took over, exuding warmth, comfort and genuine interest in the young people's lives. With the ubiquitous gaggle of hangers-on filling the space around our little circle, he managed somehow to bring all the ex-dropouts into the conversation, picking their names off their name tags, asking about their pasts and their futures, making all the worrying and the preparation that had gone into our session seem needless.

When he left, on the tick of his schedule, for yet another in the gruelling round of engagements crammed into his short stay in Toronto, about all the young people wanted to talk about was how easy he'd made the session for them, and about all the rest of us who'd met him wanted to do was marvel at how good he is at his unenviable, if financially rewarding, job.

Which includes, I guess, hearing all the stupid things we get to say to him.

PEEL, QUARTER, BOIL, MASH

❧

In a world of tiramisu, sun-dried tomatoes and edible flowers, all of which he has come to like (well, maybe not the flowers), the Aging Voluptuary still has a soft spot in his curmudgeonly heart for some of the simplest foods on earth. Nearly all of them, he realizes as he gazes on the library of cookbooks that adorn his fancy new designer kitchen, are foods that require virtually no skill and no energy to prepare. Furthermore, they're cheap; you could buy about a month's supply of any of them for just the cost of the spices in one slab of blackened red snapper.

Iceberg lettuce, for example. This is heresy to his trendy friends, whose salad components sound like the three stars of soccer night in Italy: arugula, escarole and radicchio. But at sandwich time, in particular, the Voluptuary settles for iceberg.

Sandwich time? The Voluptuary's idea of perfection is one egg fried in butter, a couple of green onions, some

Worcestershire sauce and two huge slices of bread, also fried (gently, gently) in still more butter. He likes peanut butter, too. Sometimes, when he has watched one too many TV programs where the host has all his ingredients prepared beforehand in little plastic bowls, he goes directly to the cupboard, takes out the peanut butter and slathers it, unaccompanied, on a piece of toasted sliced white bread, which he washes down with a glass of icy milk.

The Voluptuary also likes Ritz crackers, Cheddar cheese, sliced tomatoes (in season, that is; he has not yet learned to love tomatoes that bounce like tennis balls), fresh peas, vanilla ice cream, tinned salmon (mushed up with onions, mayonnaise and ground pepper), tinned consommé and tinned corn, though not, of course, as much as he likes corn on the cob, picked in the morning, boiled or barbecued in the afternoon and dripping with—here it is again—butter.

But highest of all on his list of unfashionable, simple, inexpensive delicacies is the potato. The voluptuary *loves* potatoes. He awaits the arrival of the new potatoes each summer with the same anticipation fashion addicts take to Paris. For himself, he likes them simply boiled, in their skins, fifteen minutes at the most, and smeared with (you guessed it) butter. He eschews such flights of fancy as Bert Greene's New Potatoes in Lemon (they're boiled first, skinned and then rolled in a warm pan of butter, lemon peel, lemon juice and chives) or Mustard (much the same technique). But he *is* partial to a dish served at his favourite cousins', in which fresh mint is chopped into a bowl of melted butter, which, at the table, is drizzled over plates of unpeeled but fork-broken new potatoes.

With mashed potatoes he is equally unassuming: peel, quarter, boil, mash, eat. James McNair, the American chef and writer, says in his authoritative new *Potato Cookbook* that you should "never subject potatoes to electric blenders or food processors; they'll whip them into glue." To which the Aging Voluptuary replies, "Pshaw." There is surely no better use for your electric mixer. Depending on his mood (and the state of his waistline), the Voluptuary adds, as he goes, milk or cream (it's a good idea to warm it first), sour cream or even cream cheese. He puts the butter on last, in dabs, and occasionally sticks the dish in the oven to brown on top. When he gets them right, they remind him of his grandmother. But are they out of fashion? Even Julee Rosso and Sheila Lukins, who practically gave the world sun-dried tomatoes and radicchio in their *Silver Palate Cookbook* and its sequels, say, "Mashed potatoes are one of the best things in life."

So, the Voluptuary thinks, are potato pancakes—latkes. He learned to make them years ago, from Sidney Katz, the great magazine writer, and though he has since read or heard a hundred variations, he still sticks with the original Katz recipe: Peel four medium potatoes and one good-sized onion. Now, start to warm some oil or chicken fat—half a cup should do you for this batch—in a heavy frying pan. While it's rising to medium high, grate the potatoes and onion into a bowl. Work quickly; potato batter changes colour. Add (this is important) half a teaspoon of baking powder, salt and pepper to taste, and enough flour—about a tablespoon—to hold the batter together. Moosh it around with a fork, and, if necessary, squeeze some of the moisture out. (When Sid Katz first told him how to do this, the Voluptuary, *naif* that he was, thought there wouldn't be *enough* moisture.) The size of the individual latkes, from poker chip to saucer, is a matter of personal taste. The Voluptuary, a Canadian, likes the happy medium: about the diameter of a coffee mug. For any size, spoon the batter into your hot oil and gently flatten each pancake with a spatula. They'll brown quickly—two or three minutes a side. All the experts say you should transfer each panful to a heated oven as it's done, but the Voluptuary has never been able to still his appetite long enough to serve the whole batch together. He just eats them as they're done, sometimes with applesauce, sometimes with sour cream. He is never disappointed.

THE AGING VOLUPTUARY also likes baked potatoes, from the oven or the barbecue—no foil, please—and scalloped potatoes: layer of peeled, sliced potatoes, layer of peeled, sliced onions, sprinkling of flour, salt and pepper, and repeat to within an inch of the top of your greased baking dish; pour in a couple of cups of hot milk, top the whole with shredded Cheddar and bake at 350°F (180°C) for an hour and a half. He likes potato soups and potato salads, roast potatoes and fried potatoes—especially, when they're "fried" in the oven: peeled, sliced as thinly as your knife can make them, spread on a baking sheet, sprinkled with just a drop or two of oil for each chip and baked lovingly (at 425°F, 220°C) till they turn to gold, about ten or fifteen minutes a side.

In recent years, he has also learned to appreciate the tins of potatoes, whole, peeled and already cooked, that are available at his local supermarket. He uses them in his famous stews and, in summer, sticks them on the barbecue, rolled first in oil and then skewered, either as a side dish on their own or as part of a kebob. He roasts them with his chickens or cuts them up (they come sliced, as well) for hash browns. They are, in fact—except when the new potatoes come in—a staple of his kitchen and his diet. But the Aging Voluptuary is reluctant to talk about that. He thinks they might be too fashionable.

Cars I Have Known
—and Tamed

જ

Just as he had promised, and just as if he did this sort of thing all the time (as, in fact, he may have), the salesman brought The Car to my front door.

"Hmm," I said. "Black, eh?"

He ran his hand over the mirrored polish of the hood. "Oh, yes," he said. "Black. Black and bee-you-ti-ful."

"Big, too," I said. "Bigger than I've ever owned."

He stepped back about three feet and aimed the ignition key at the door lock. He pressed down with his thumb. Something clicked. The door unlocked itself. "Want to go for a spin?" he said.

I slid onto the upholstered driver's seat, soft as a monarch's divan, and at the salesman's instruction pushed a button or two to adjust height, angle and distance from the wheel.

Half an hour later, half an hour of gliding over country roads—"Keep the cruise control on unless you go too fast," my co-pilot said seductively—with the motor purring under the symphony of the FM, with the computer-controlled air wafting about my ears and the power steering responsive to my every whim, I knew I was in for more than I could afford.

Or, if the truth be told, live up to.

I AM NOT A CAR PERSON. I don't understand cars. I can't fix them—I can handle a flat, if necessary, and, in the old days at least, knew what to do when the fan belt was loose—and don't much like talking about them. I'm not car proud, either; no one's ever seen me whiling away a Saturday afternoon with a hose and chamois or, for that matter, caught me inside a commercial car wash.

I'm tougher on cars than I should be, too. My ashtrays (for shame) overflow, and stuff piles up on the seats. Nearly everything I've driven for more than a year has shown the wear and tear of my enthusiastic driving. But I've *liked* the cars I've driven over the years, and taken pleasure from their personalities.

When I was young, I bought a young man's cars. My first—our first cars live as long in our memories as our first loves—was a nifty little Austin convertible, green as lime sherbet. I bought it—well, I and my close friends at Household Finance bought it—for eight hundred dollars, in Moose Jaw, where I had my first permanent job. I drove it all one prairie summer, commuting under the stars back and forth to Regina, with only the single curve over the railroad tracks at Belle Plain to break the monotony, to court the woman I later married. We drove that Austin east, too—or almost. We took a short cut down through Michigan, and somewhere around Bay City, the points (I think) welded themselves together, and the best mechanics of the automotive state couldn't figure out what made that little English sewing machine run.

Then a Nash. Not the famous Rambler of the fifties and sixties, but a Metropolitan, red as a cherry, a two-seater, so thin it looked as if a giant had squeezed it between his hands. It was *streamlined,* man. I drove my Metropolitan a long time, too, giving up on it only when (a) we started needing room for baby seats and (b) we moved to Montreal, where the traffic terrified me. That year, kids and all, we relied on taxis.

Back in Toronto, and still at least *feeling* young, I found yet another convertible, this one big enough to handle our growing family: a pale blue Oldsmobile Cutlass with white leather seats and, miracle of miracles, a top that went up mechanically. And then, giving in at last to the realities of the Canadian winter and the need for a real city car, we picked up a small and practical Datsun—except that it was as red as my old Nash had been, and had four-on-the-floor to make the driving more fun. Vroom, vroom.

I DIDN'T BUY my first serious car until about fifteen years ago, when I fled the city and took up life as a country mouse. Since the mouse still had to go into town most days, and that meant spending a minimum of two hours behind the wheel, I bought the first of what was to become a series of good, solid, dependable machines, on which the money was spent on efficiency. There was, for instance, no power steering, and if you wanted to open the window you cranked it by hand.

And then, this year, I decided to go for broke. Why not? The kids were finished their educations, the mortgage on the cottage was all but paid off, and I—well, I guess I felt like a change.

THREE DAYS AFTER my test drive, the salesman came back with The Car. This time, he brought a colleague in a second vehicle. When he left, The Car would be mine.

For most of an hour, we sat at the kitchen table, going over not only the requisite paperwork, but the owner's manual and instructions. Then, for most of *another* hour, we sat in The Car itself, while he took me through its various features: the variable-speed windshield wipers; the front seat heaters; the computerized temperature control, which makes—and shows you on a little screen—its own decisions about how much fan and how much intake; the thief- (and just possibly owner-) proof security system; the tape deck's ability to find your favourite song; the windows that open at a touch of your pinkie; the memory to do this, the program to . . .

"And, oh," said the salesman before he departed. "Do you think you could park it somewhere else? The sap from that tree will fall right on the black finish."

I was almost totally depressed.

The Car, I thought, is smarter than I am. You can't even leave the *lights* on overnight; when you open the front door, they turn themselves off.

The salesman shook my hand, turned over the key

with its mysterious remote-control function and drove off into the evening.

I slid behind the wheel and started her up.

Then, heading for my maiden voyage of command, I backed into the wooden box where the garbage waits for collection, and gouged a white scrape into the immaculate finish of the left rear fender.

CHEEK TO CHEEK

W HEN CHI CHI RODRIGUEZ issued his dictum that "the older we get, the better we used to be," he was talking about golf, the game he plays for a living. He was right, too, as my own adventures on the links attest. I now spend most of my time slicing balls out of bounds and excavating divots the size of dinner plates, explaining (falsely) that, listen, when I was a kid I'd have hit that green with a drive and a seven iron.

Chi Chi would have been even more correct, though—at least in my case—if he'd addressed himself to dancing. As a lithe teenager (or so I am convinced) I could whirl and twirl with the best of them: the foxtrot, the tango (remember the slide and "dancing balmy"?), the waltz (well, maybe not the waltz), even, from time to time, the reckless abandon of jiving.

But not now, my dears, not now. Creaky of joint and paralyzed by self-consciousness, I have become that solitary last male at the table, sipping morosely at his

postprandial wine, avoiding the glances of the last solitary
female, whose partner is shaking his booty (whatever a
booty is) with the woman who'd been sitting next to me.

Except for a couple of times when forces beyond my
control have taken over, I haven't been on my feet since
Chubby Checker sat down at the piano.

And yet, there I was, standing at a podium at the Red
Barn theatre in Jackson's Point, Ontario, my palms
sweaty, my knees atremble, the piano magic of Hagood
Hardy pulsing in the air.

Climbing the steps to the stage, smiling radiantly,
was one of the great ballerinas in the history of North
America, a former partner of Nureyev and Baryshnikov.
And when she got there, as the audience in its happy
ignorance was not expecting, I was supposed to . . . supposed to—oh, sweet Terpsichore, say it isn't so—I was
supposed to *dance* with her.

Actually, the force was beyond my control this time,
too. The force's name was Carole Warren. Carole, as well
as a friend, was a colleague at CBC radio, and I had asked
her to help organize an evening at the Red Barn to cele-
brate the fifth anniversary of the golf tournaments held in
my name for literacy. When she signed on, the evening
was to have consisted only of a barbecue and a few readings and songs by people who'd played golf with us over
the years. With Carole on board, our plans grew. The list
of readers spread to include such literary stars as June
Callwood, W. O. Mitchell and Timothy Findley. Dianne
Heatherington, Mary Lou Fallis (surely the funniest
soprano in the world), Dinah Christie, Tom Kneebone,

Murray McLauchlan and Tom Cochrane all agreed to sing. Hagood Hardy would play the piano. And—this is when I should have seen it coming—Veronica Tennant, the retired superstar of the National Ballet, would dance.

"She thinks you should be her partner," Carole said.

"Are you both out of your minds?" I said.

THE OTHER TWO TIMES I had danced had involved golfing for literacy, as well.

In April, a whole gang of us, thanks to the generosity of such sponsors as Air Canada, Canada Post and Southam News, had raised $110,000 for Arctic literacy by playing on an ice course at Yellowknife. On our arrival, we'd been whisked across Great Slave Lake to a Dene village for an evening of traditional dancing. The forces that got me this time were the hypnotic rhythms of the drums and the fact that every one of my fellow travellers—from the athletes Ken Dryden and Michael Smith to Cynthia Dale of *Street Legal*—was already out on the floor.

Then, on the eve of our third Ottawa tournament, the Department of the Secretary of State threw us a reception in the National Press Club. The year before, Wayne Rostad, the country singer and TV host, had raised several hundred extra dollars by getting the audience to chip in to hear me sing—which I do, if anything, even more atrociously than I waltz. This year, I extracted from Wayne a promise of no singing. "No problem," he said. Then he summoned both me and our host, the Hon. Gerry Weiner, to the centre of the floor, told us to doff our jackets, twanged out a lively Ottawa Valley jig on his guitar and—you guessed it—the Hon. Gerry and I made fools of ourselves.

"JUST TRUST ME," Carole Warren had said. "Or, if not, trust Veronica. She knows what she's doing. We'll have a rehearsal in the radio building and—"

"A *rehearsal*," I had choked. "Even Wayne Rostad—"

"Trust me," Carole repeated.

NOW I STOOD at the podium. At the piano, Hagood, having finished his solo turn, ran arpeggio after arpeggio, as if refusing to go off. A book was open before me. I pretended I was going to read.

As Veronica reached the top of the steps, Hagood swung into the bounce of "Cheek to Cheek."

Veronica danced once around the stage, as sublime as ever. Then—exactly as we had rehearsed it—she reached out her lovely arm for me.

I wished for a trap door.

But you know something? I made it. Not well, mind you—*believe* me, not well—but the incomparable Tennant guided me with her movements and the words she whispered through her smile ("And now the kick part") right to the last bar, when, after a cheek-to-cheek glide to centre stage, Veronica dropped gracefully backward and, somehow, arranged for me to catch her in a classic pose.

Phew! People laughed and—honestly!—clapped with pleasure. If only, I thought for one intoxicating moment, I'd known Veronica Tennant back when I used to tango.

Nah. She probably couldn't have kept up with me.

IF IT LOOKS LIKE BORSCHT
AND IT TASTES
LIKE BORSCHT . . .

❧

THE AGING VOLUPTUARY often appears to cook off the top of his head—to begin each new adventure in the kitchen by checking the refrigerator and the cupboards and then to make up, as best he can, a dish to suit what's available.

When he is alone, this is true. But at heart the Voluptuary is a cookbook man. His shelves are lined with books on food. He reads them for pleasure—he likes nothing better than to drift to sleep over Laurie Colwin's evocation of pot roast or Roy Andries de Groot's travels in provincial France—and he gives them as gifts. He gathers cookbooks as souvenirs and he browses through them to refresh his memory—sometimes of places he has never been. And most of all, he cooks with them.

Not slavishly. The Voluptuary will cheerfully omit the apples from *Harrowsmith*'s red cabbage and apples (he never remembers to buy apples anyway) and add caraway seeds instead—though the caraway seeds, to be honest, come from *The New Basics Cookbook*. He will sauté onions where the recipe calls for caramelizing (he thinks all food writers fry their onions too long), pour the butter into his hollandaise instead of drizzling it, leave the skins on tomatoes, change spices at will (whoever has cumin anyway?), and, without even a test run, use three times the garlic prescribed by even such authorities as the editors of his own beloved *Canadian Living*.

But he is still a follower. He began his cooking career by tentatively making onion soup from a paperback called *The Art of French Cooking*—scalded milk was the secret— and now, a quarter of a century later, he never tries anything new without an exploratory browse through his library. Even the recipes for which he is world famous—or world famous among his friends—started in someone else's book: his potatoes-in-foil with Bonnie Stern, his pork tenderloin and morels with Joanne Kates, his incomparable fried egg sandwich (chopped scallions sautéed in butter, one egg over lightly with a dollop of Worcestershire sauce in its yoke, one side of each of two slabs of French bread bronzed in still more butter) came from a book of Wisconsin cooking he has long since outgrown.

And some days he longs to be free.

A WINTER SATURDAY. Guests are coming. The Voluptuary is way ahead of schedule. He has cleaned and chopped the wing tips from a free-range chicken. He has stuffed its cavity with—this from the *Joy of Cooking*, but with much liberty—leeks, celery heart, bread crumbs, pecans, thyme, rosemary, sage, chopped garlic, pepper and salt. He has opened a tin of whole potatoes and will spread them around the chicken while it roasts, ready for basting in the sizzling fat. Slim asparagus lies in a pan of chicken stock, awaiting the microwave. The guests, good friends, will bring dessert. It's still early afternoon, and he has time for a crowning touch.

What is needed, he thinks, is a soup. With the heartiness of the main course, a chilled soup—the Aging Voluptuary prides himself on his chilled soups—would be sublime. The Voluptuary has it: borscht!

There are beets. More of the powdered chicken stock in which he'll nuke the asparagus. Sour cream. Milk. Hmm. What else? He checks his indispensable *Greene on Greens*, a large and (in the AV's house well-thumbed) paperback by the redoubtable American chef Bert Greene. There we are: page 47, with the arc of half a soup pot's bottom proof that the Voluptuary has been here before.

But what is this? Greene calls for cucumber. And the Voluptuary, now in happy reverie over the prospect of a pink overture to the green and golden meal that lies ahead, has no cukes.

His shoulders droop. But, resolutely, he soldiers on. He brings a pound of the beets to the boil and simmers them for half an hour. Drains and peels them. Runs them through the food processor with the garlic—three cloves instead of Greene's one. Mixes in a couple of cups of chicken stock, a cup of milk and more than one of sour cream. Before setting the mixture in to chill, he tastes it. It is beet soup, he thinks, but it is not borscht. He sighs audibly, and wonders about starting again.

AND NOW Gill enters the picture. She is best known in these pages for her skills as a gardener, but she cooks, too. But where the Voluptuary putters and pronounces, she just gets on with the job. Furthermore, to his knowledge, she has never opened a cookbook in her life.

"What's the problem?" she asks her sulking partner. He tells her.

"Let me taste," she says brightly.

"There are no cucum—"

"Horseradish," she says.

"Horseradish?" barks the Voluptuary. "In my *soup?* No cookbook I've ever seen says—"

"Horseradish," says Gill.

Together, they add a tablespoon. Another. She tastes.

"More," she says. Another and still another.

Now the Voluptuary tastes. The soup is tangy, the flavour of the beets enhanced, the pink seductively pale. It is—he admits it readily now—wonderful. It is *borscht.*

The Aging Voluptuary looks at his bulging shelf of cookbooks, and contemplates the limits of the written word.

My Six Religious

ॐ

I WAS LATE FOR DINNER—I had messed up my instructions—and when the taxi pulled up at the curb in Toronto's Parkdale district, I was fluttering with nerves.

"Are you *sure* it's over there?" I asked the driver, giving the street number.

"Gotta be one of those," he said, pointing across the tree-lined street. It was Grey Cup night. He was anxious to get back downtown.

I overtipped him, gathered up my two bottles of wine and the copy of my latest book, a gift for the hostess, and clambered out.

I was more apprehensive than I'd been since Christmas 1946, when Jane Roelofson, who could figure skate, invited me home to meet her parents.

I could make out the street numbers from the sidewalk. Light shone through the leaded glass of the doorway. A hospitable glow lit the bay windows to my left.

I rang the bell.

Two of my six blind dates came to answer the door.
I wondered which one was the nun.

THIS ALL STARTED last fall in the column in which I
imagined having a fantasy dinner with ten women I
knew, or knew about, from (alphabetically), Mary
Wynne Ashford, the doctor who heads the Canadian
Physicians for the Prevention of Nuclear War, to Margaret Somerville, the lawyer and Ph.D. who runs the
Institute for Medicine, Ethics and the Law at McGill.

I enjoyed writing that column—who wouldn't?—and
its reception. But something nagged at me. All my
"guests"—Barbara *McDougall* was on the list, for heaven's
sake—were women you might have read about in the
newspapers. I wondered if I'd sent a message that the only
people I'd find interesting enough to spend an evening
with, even if only in my imagination, were those who'd
made headlines.

If I had, I'd have been wrong. Some of the most attractive, interesting and—to use the criteria I mentioned
in drawing up my list—"bright and cheeky" women I
know spend most of their time around the house or, if
not, in out-of-the-house jobs that don't make the
papers. I wished, somehow, my dinner-date column had
made that clear.

Which is where the letter I received from southern
Ontario comes in. It said, among other things, "Six of us
would like to throw a dinner party for *you.* . . . We don't
have the high-profile credentials of the women on your
list, but we do have a love of life and a passion for many of

the concerns and issues that emerged in the article," and it went on to spell out some of the vocations the author and her friends pursued, from religious education to the teaching of theology. They were all Catholics. One was a Sister. "We're not religious nuts," the letter said.

And, on Grey Cup night, there I was, standing on the veranda, my wine and my paperback under my arm, fidgety as an altar boy.

"SO WHY DID YOU do this, anyway?"

The ice was broken now. In the living room whose warm light I had perceived from the porch, my four other dates had awaited. Over paté and cheese, we had begun to get to know each other. One of the women who'd come to the door, it turned out, *was* the Sister, although, rather than a habit, she wore a calf-length skirt, black stockings and a long-sleeved white blouse. Most of the others— two former nuns, I learned, as well as a couple of wives and mothers—were, as the letter had said, involved in education.

At the beginning, they'd been as self-conscious as I. But when we'd started talking about their work in the schools, and about a panel of young people we'd had on *Morningside* the week before, and my dates' universal belief that the kids they worked with needed better—and not necessarily better *religious*—guidance on sex, we'd found common ground. As with all good dinner parties, the conversation had a life of its own. By the time we moved to the dining room, frank questions were in order, including the one I'd just been asked.

"I'm not sure," I said. "In spite of being on the radio every day—where, truth to tell, I can hide behind the microphone while I ask impertinent questions—I'm shy in public, uncomfortable with strangers. I just thought I would . . . oh, just do this once."

"Well, how do you think *we* felt when you said you'd come?" said the author of the original letter, one of the former nuns. "It was just one of those letters you feel like writing."

"Uh . . . do you think I might have just a bit more of that chicken piccata?" I said. "It's delicious."

I STAYED MUCH LATER than I had intended. Over the piccata, buttery carrots and wild rice, green beans and almonds, we talked about the changing church (anyone who thinks the current Pope speaks for modern, female Canadian Catholics on such issues as birth control, abortion and the ordination of women—"I'd still be in if I could have been a priest," someone said—should spend some time with *my* six religious), about cooking (I learned how to coddle an egg), about teaching French, Quebec's language law, raising daughters, why single women in Toronto these days seem to outnumber available men, about kids who think Sisters don't wear underwear, about inconsiderate smokers ("Go ahead and light up," said my hostess, bringing an ashtray to the table, "but two's your limit indoors"), golf, literacy, the CBC, love, life, wine and my perfect granddaughter. When we'd polished off a fluffy chocolate cake, one of the former sisters—the one who'd told a hilarious story about giving the sermon in my old boarding school—brought out some Grand Marnier, and before I left, we all went into the study in the big old house to watch the thrilling last minutes of the Grey Cup.

When, at last, I left, my six dates walked me across the frozen lawn, and as the cab idled impatiently in the background, we all shook hands. As I trundled back downtown, I wondered if, had my own fantasy guests been able to accept my public invitation, I'd have had so lovely a time.

Waiting for Joe

WHOSE IDEA IT WAS that we should put Joe Clark—
that's the Right Honorable Joe Clark, as in former prime
minister of Canada—into a *variety* show in the first place,
I'm not sure. I know it came early in our planning. Summer was looming. Soon we'd hit the road with the
combinations of celebration and golf that raise funds for
literacy all over the country, and we'd start, once again, in
the Red Barn theatre at my home course at Lake Simcoe,
in Ontario.

Our Red Barn evenings are like old-fashioned village
concerts. After a barbecue, everyone just strolls into the
theatre while some singers and dancers and writers—
including, always, at least one person who's learned to
read through money we've raised—take the stage to read
or perform. But, over the years, we've always tried to
build in a surprise or two: Veronica Tennant coming out
of the audience to whisk me away in a few ballet steps, for

example, or David Peterson appearing to turn the pages of a piano score for Bob Rae.

And this year, someone suggested, let's have Joe Clark. Why not, I said. He's very popular now (this was just after he'd announced his resignation from politics) and no one would see it as a partisan gesture. And, heaven knows, if we could sneak him past the barbecuers and walk him on between, say, Buffy Saint-Marie and our poet, he'd certainly be a surprise.

Furthermore, I'd had some contact with Mr. Clark—Joe, as I guess I once knew him—in times past. Once, when he was waiting to do an interview on *Morningside*, he told me disarmingly that just after he'd finished university and I was a cocky young editor at *Maclean's*, I'd turned him down for a job. Before that, just after he'd become leader of his party, he'd been a very casual guest on my late-night television program, and, like a lot of Canadians of all political stripes, I'd felt he'd had a rough deal in public office—beginning in 1979 when his government, in a snap vote in the House, slipped through his fingers.

In any case, I'd have no trouble making the request. When I did, to our delight, he agreed—element of surprise and all.

Then we *really* began our preparations.

Two of the other people we had asked to appear at the Barn, both friends from the CBC, were Ralph Benmergui and Ernie Coombs, better known, of course (to *millions* of Canadians), as Mr. Dress-Up.

When Joe Clark agreed to join us, we drafted a skit around him.

First, I'd appear on stage to say that the CBC had finally solved its late-night problems (Ralph still hadn't been renewed). Then, from backstage, you'd hear, "It's Friday Night with . . . Mr. Dress-Up." We'd play that familiar tinkly theme, Ernie would appear in garish clothes, do a monologue ("This kitten goes into a bar . . ."), introduce his first guest—Ralph—and, after some banter, Ralph would tell Ernie that what his show needed was some political content.

Getting it yet?

What we figured is Ralph would say something like, "Let me help you. I'll be . . . oh, say, Joe Clark," and, in a mock interview, he'd break into a not-very-good imitation.

And then, by assembling some tape clips, we'd have some other impressionists say, one by one, "No, no, *that's* not the way you do Joe Clark," building to the moment when Joe himself would walk out and show them how it's really done.

Pretty funny, eh? Well, if not, at least surprising. And Mr. Clark, or so his office told us, loved it.

Except that now, here it was, the day before the barbecue, with everything in place—line-up done, taped impressions assembled, precautions in place to hide our punch line and—

—and I was on the phone with Ottawa.

The minister couldn't make it.

His staff couldn't have been nicer. Mr. Clark was as disappointed as we were, they said. Only a firm order from the prime minister's office that all cabinet ministers and

MPs stay in Ottawa for an emergency vote of confidence in the Commons had made them change their plans. Why, Mr. Clark had even picked out a piece of a Wallace Stegner novel to read as his contribution to literacy.

In desperation, we tried some last-minute revisions. Jean Chretien was due to play golf with us the next day; maybe he could . . . No, his office said, he'd get in much too late. Maybe *Wendel* Clark of the Toronto Maple Leafs, who had just ended their gallant run at the Stanley Cup, could say, "Well, I'm not Joe, but . . ." No, his agent said, Wendel had left for Saskatchewan.

That evening, as we worked out a whole new premise for our late-night skit, Joe Clark called me at home.

He was, as he has always been with me, decent and affable—and, again, very apologetic.

It was only the vote of confidence that kept him away, he said. With the Tory leadership campaign in full sway, the opposition was going to try to pull a fast one.

"Gee, Minister," I said, "I don't think our literacy programs have ever held the fate of a government in their hands before."

"Well," said Joe Clark, with the self-deprecating chuckle we never did get to imitate, "I have."

ELLY, NOT ALONE

∾

I AM UPSTAIRS in the Grand Theatre in Kingston,
Ontario, in a room rented for the evening by the owners
of an ambitious bookstore. I have read aloud from my
latest book and now—the true purpose of this curious
ritual—the people who have come to hear me are lined
up before the table where I wait to sign the copies they
have dutifully bought.

A woman about forty, dressed neatly but in drab
colours, reaches the front of the line. She has no book to
be signed, only a message. She speaks softly, so the others
in the line-up do not hear.

"Thank you for Elly," she says.

I look up, my pen stilled. She swallows, and forces a
smile.

"It gave me the courage to—to do what I had to do,"
she says. She turns to leave. As gently as I can, I call her
back.

"Did you just tell me what I thought you told me?" I ask. "You, too?"

"Yes," she says, "me, too," and, smiling strongly now, she makes her exit from the scene.

ELLY CAME INTO my life almost by coincidence. But when I think of what effects our meeting had, I am tempted to wonder if there wasn't something more at work—a fate, perhaps, or a divine power that determined her story be told as widely as it could. For if there were thanks to be offered by the people who found inspiration in what she offered, they were certainly not due to me.

She had written a book about what had happened to her, a slim paperback, ninety-six pages in all, published by "gynergy books," an obscure publishing house based in Prince Edward Island. Elly's book—Elly Danica is her full name—is called simply *Don't: A Woman's Word*. On its cover the word *Don't* is printed twelve times, at first small, in a light grey type, and then larger and darker until, at the bottom of the page, you can almost feel her scream of terror.

Don't was published in the summer. Though a copy had been forwarded to *Morningside*, I was away when it arrived, and it fell unnoticed among the steady stream of books that come into our office in Toronto, each one seeking some publicity for its author.

Then, in late autumn, I published a book of my own, and was planning to take to the road to promote it. My first sortie was to be to Saskatchewan. Some of the scenes in my book are set in Moose Jaw, where I had worked as a young newspaperman. The Moose Jaw Chamber of Commerce had invited me to speak to them, and the opportunity to read some of the Saskatchewan scenes to them was too good to resist. At the same time, the producers with whom I work at the CBC, where we are always short of travel money, planned to use my trip, which would be paid for by the Chamber of Commerce, to tape some interviews away from our Toronto studio.

Just before we were due to leave, a second copy of Elly's book arrived in the mail. I might have ignored it again—by autumn, the torrent of books at *Morningside* reaches an unmanageable crescendo—except that a letter in the same package said, among other things, "Do you know the events described in this book took place in Moose Jaw about the same time as you were there, and that you might have known some of the men involved?"

Intrigued, I began to read. Once started, I couldn't stop. For all its unpretentious package, *Don't: A Woman's Word* turned out to be both horrifying and hauntingly beautiful. Tightly written to the point of poetry—as if each sentence has been boiled down to its essence—it tells the story of the unspeakable sexual invasion of a child. The child is, or was, Elly. The invasion is conducted by her father and his friends, a group of otherwise "respectable" citizens of the town where she grew up, and who might well have been, as the writer of the letter had said, people I had met around the town, for, although the book never names it, Moose Jaw is where it's set. To take only one of the horrors described in stark and boiled-down text: Elly's father took pornographic pictures of her, aged nine, and sold them to his friends.

Beautiful? Only in this way: Elly has triumphed over her past. After a life sent spinning by the hell of her child-hood, and without the help that would have been available to her in a better world, she holed up in an old prairie church, which she rented for a pittance, and read—and wrote—her way back to sanity.

It was in that church that my producers and I found her, and arranged to visit after we had wrapped up our Moose Jaw excursion. She is about forty now, perhaps the same age as the woman I met in Kingston, slight, pert, still vulnerable. If you want to hug her, you warn her first—she still instinctively shrinks from the touch of a man.

In the basement of the church, surrounded by some of the books she read to help her in her struggle, she told her story again, on tape. Not all of it, to be sure, for there are passages in what she has written she still cannot read aloud or speak about. But the courage with which she has con-quered her past was in her voice as we talked and, later, when we came to broadcast our interview on *Morning-side,* we filled in the details with readings by the actress Susan Hogan.

The woman in Kingston was not alone.

I have done *Morningside* for nearly seven years now, two hundred programs a year, perhaps a dozen interviews a day, somewhere in the tens of thousands of pieces of radio. While others have drawn more mail or more public comment or won us more recognition or awards, none, I am convinced, of those thousands of items has had a more direct and powerful impact on the people who heard it, including those who told us later they had wanted to turn it off but couldn't. Telling her story—a much more common one than we are prepared to admit to ourselves—Elly helped to cast one more shaft of light into this dark and squalid corner of our lives. Perhaps most important of all, she let a lot of other women (and some men) know they were not alone, and that there might be help for them, if only in their own strengths.

All of that, as I did not have time to tell the woman in Kingston, because of one small coincidence that started in the morning mail.

ENVOI

REVENGE OF THE TREE
AND OTHER POSTSCRIPTS

ॐ

SUMMER. A Sunday evening. Gill, with a day job to go to in the morning, has left for the city. A solitary dinner lies ahead.

This book—at last, I want to say, for the work, however pleasant, has stretched out—is all but finished. On Friday, the editors gathered here for one last merry meeting, and all weekend the people and the places of the past five years have filtered in and out of my mind.

LONG AFTER I WROTE about her, Elly Danica, whose story we chose to end with, remains a presence in my life.

I saw her just a few weeks ago, looking better, I couldn't help noting, than I've ever seen her—not plump certainly, but less sparrow-like than she used to be, less frail. When we talked for the radio, there was sunshine in her voice.

Her healing goes on. It may not—probably will not—

ever be complete; the scars are too deep. But, as I know from so many other occasions that have paralleled the one at the Kingston book-signing, the healing works not only within her but from her, and, as she has made her way around the country—she is an important figure in the fight against sexual abuse now—she's helped countless other women deal with their pain.

As we left the studio this time, Elly gave *me* a hug.

I SHOULD START on dinner. But, like the Aging Voluptuary, whom I created on an evening such as this, I am still not convinced that eating alone is eating for pleasure. It feels like work. Let it wait.

I HAVE YET TO HUG—or, indeed, meet in person—Dennis Kaye, the Incredible Shrinking Man. I continue to hear from him, though, most recently just after he'd sent off the manuscript of *his* book to *his* publisher. Bravo!

Whatever the state of his wordly flesh, Dennis's spirit remains indomitable. He may yet outlast us all.

I WISH I COULD BE as optimistic about The Tree, which grows more desolate with every passing season, as I am about Dennis.

The green has gone from all its upper branches now, and lower down—we conducted some triage last year—The Tree seems to sense its own impending death.

Before it goes, and gives way to more of Gill's ever-expanding garden it's having its revenge.

The Car, monument to my self-indulgence, now sleeps under what's left of its shelter. Steadily, and especially in summer, a mysterious white gunk oozes from the decaying branches. As a result, the once-gleaming surface of The Car now looks—always—as if I have just driven it under a squadron of Stuka dive-pigeons.

The irremovable white smears, however, fail to cover the tell-tale scar on its left rear fender—or the even longer one I engraved on the other side a week or so later, just to match things up.

THERE IS A STEAK, I remember. Alex the butcher—who still won't sell me lamb without an argument—threw an extra one in last week. I *could* fire up the barbecue, and. . .

MY GOLF TOURNAMENTS for literacy roll on. They continue to take me into each province and into each northern territory at least once a year. Even without the $2 million or so they've raised for literacy, they would have been worthwhile for me. They restore me, and provide a constant reminder of the endless variety and aching beauty of the land.

And look at the people I've come to know: Valdy and Tom Jackson, Cynthia Dale and Murray McLauchlan, Joe Ghiz (out of politics now, but not, a bunch of us learned at his house last month, out of the Caesar salad business) and Anne Meekitjuk Hansen. So many others. . . . And Pond Inlet. Would I ever have been to Pond if. . . ?

I'll be sixty years old next summer, and every year it

gets a little harder to take off from, if I may quote myself, the hedges and the cedars and the peace. But I'll miss the friendships if I stop, and the travel.

BEFORE THE BARBECUE IS READY for the steak, I *could* roast that last red pepper (you don't need to let them sweat, you know; just blacken them and when they're ready, peel 'em). And weren't there some mushrooms in the fridge? I could saute them in (of course) butter, with some garlic and—my specialty—a spritz of lemon juice and . . .

IN THE SUMMER after I published my list of fantasy dinner companions, my oldest son called to say that if I'd care to drive down to Toronto on my birthday, the kids would like to throw me a little dinner party.

"Where?" I said.

"Oh, a restaurant we know. It's a bit of a surprise."

We met at Yonge and Eglinton. They walked me down Holly Street.

"This is nice," I said, catching up on my granddaughter's latest accomplishments as we strolled. "Did you know this is where *Canadian Living* has its offices?"

"Relax," said John.

I was still preoccupied with Stephanie when we turned towards the building where I send my columns. Didn't twig, in fact, until we were in the lobby and I noticed that the receptionist bore a startling resemblance to Dinah Chr—holy smoke, *was* Dinah Christie, and that the woman in the straw hat *was* Barbara McDougall, and that. . .

They were all there—all except Evelyn Hart, who would have come if she could, she'd told the others, except she was dancing in Munich. They'd come on their own, many of them using hard-earned travel points, as curious as I was, I suppose, to see what dinner would be like. Nellie Cournoyea brought a muskrat (country food again) which she skinned and boiled before our real dinner, which was lamb, prepared under the supervision of the incomparable Elizabeth Baird. Mary-Wynne Ashford and Dulcie McCallum brought nostrums from the west, Margaret Somerville from Montreal and—well, enough, except to say that Debbie Brill, the high jumper, presented me with an elegant, framed image, which might have been two red avocados on a background of white, but turned out to be, when Debbie ended the guessing game, the world's most beautiful—and now most cherished—self-made bum-print.

The dinner?

I have, if I may say so, terrific taste in dinner companions, chimerical or, as came to pass, real.

THREE SUMMERS LATER, I met Clarence Asham, the musical savant from Winnipeg. He came to play his accordion at—yes—a golf-related event.

In person, Clarence turned out to be as sweet as he'd been on the radio. He remembered our earlier conversation, and, as he shook my hand and repeated my name, added the same phrase he'd used then as a sign of recognition: "Nine-thirty in Newfoundland."

Some psychologists, I learned, had taken him a while ago to his first-ever live symphony concert. They wanted to see if there was a limit to the amount of classical music Clarence could absorb on first hearing and recreate. And so, almost immediately after the concert, they sat him at a piano and asked him to play what he remembered.

Disaster—or so everyone was convinced.

Instead of playing the music he had heard, Clarence seemed to be hitting notes at random. Atonal, non-harmonic chaos.

The experts looked at each other in dismay.

And then, after five minutes of musical gibberish, Clarence without warning switched to recognizable chord patterns and melodies. The evening's concert began to flow from his piano.

Finally the people round him realized what had happened.

Clarence Asham, whose IQ had once been measured at thirty-eight, had stored in his mind not only the evening's program but the sound of the orchestra tuning up.

No one, you see, had told him it wasn't music.

I LIGHT THE BARBECUE. Dinner will be a pleasure after all.

Maybe, I think, I'll take some notes as I go. Bonnie is expecting a column soon, and, as I've learned, you never know where one is going to turn up.

Colophon

THE TEXT TYPE that appears in this book is Bembo. This face has been drawn from the designs of Francesco Griffo [*c.* 1450-1518]. The excellence of Griffo's design became the model for the great French type designers of the sixteenth century. ¶ The display type is Trump Mediaeval, drawn from the designs of Georg Trump [*b.* 1896], one of the Stuttgart School's most accomplished typographers. ¶ The type has been electronically set in-house by the publishers, from manuscript provided on-disc by the author. ¶ The wood engravings found throughout the book are details from Gerard Brender à Brandis's *Garden Triptych* [1987]. ¶ The book has been printed in Canada on archival papers.

DESIGN BY PETER SIBBALD BROWN